More praise for *I, Witness*

"A page-turning glimpse into the lifestyle of a Jehovah's Witness. In sharing his memoir, Clark seeks catharsis and closure. Clark's portrayal of the life of a Jehovah's Witness is grounded in a lifelong experience with this often-mysterious faith; anyone who has received a Witness at their door will find Clark's perspective intriguing. The story is engrossing, and the writing solid. One man's successful return from a spiritual hell."

—*Kirkus Discoveries*

"Sure to be controversial and shocking. Clark's account of his personal experiences with Jehovah's Witnesses is unnerving and oftentimes shattering. It's an important book that will be sure to stir a lot of discussion."

—Janette Owens, author of *Man With a Vengeance*

"Brilliantly written, the author's experience with the Watchtower Society is both raw and riveting. Highly recommended."

—Vivekanand Palavali, M.D. author of *A Mindful Life*

I, Witness

The Shocking Insider's
Story of Jehovah's Witnesses

I, Witness

The Shocking Insider's
Story of Jehovah's Witnesses

Daniel Clark

Villa Press

For further information, please contact:

Villa Press
P.O. Box 4841
Englewood, CO 80155-4841

Website Address: www.villapress.com (U.S. Inquiries)
                  www.villapress.cn (International Inquiries)

E-mail Address: sales@villapress.com
                  info@villapress.com

Book design by:
Arbor Books, Inc.
www.arborbooks.com

Printed in the United States

I, Witness: The Shocking Insider's Story of Jehovah's Witnesses
Daniel Clark

1. Title 2. Author 3. Christianity/Jehovah's Witnesses

Library of Congress Control Number: 2007924809

ISBN 10: 0-9794637-0-X
ISBN 13: 978-0-9794637-0-9

But seek first the kingdom of God and His righteousness,
and all these things shall be added to you.
—Jesus Christ, Matthew 6:32-34 (New King James Bible)

Acknowledgements

First of all, I'd like to thank Almighty God for the unconditional love extended to me, sending me many, many "angels" in people to assist me through my journey.

I would like to say thank you to Marsha Hansen for her endless self sacraficing love. She taught me so many things; all about co-dependency, assertiveness, all sorts of religious recovery techniques, how to be responsible and okay with myself, how to love myself and others unconditionally and so much more! Marsha, how can I ever thank you enough for all that you did for me. I love you.

I'd like to thank Dennis Church—a real modern day good samaritan. It's wonderful to me that there are people like Dennis that will offer a complete stranger a hand up just because it's the right thing to do (I certainly needed it at the time). Thank you Dennis.

I'd also like to thank Dave French for his constant positive attitude toward life and for believing in me when I didn't believe in myself. Everybody needs and deserves a friend like Dave.

I would also like to thank Maya Bohnhoff for her creative help and assistance in writing this book. Without her, I don't believe this book would have been written. Maya, you are very talented and very appreciated. I could say so much more. Thank You!

Finally, I can't say enough about my wife, Angela. She takes my breath away. She carries with her the love of God. Thanks for all the hours of typing, editing, emails, filing and organizing. Thanks for all of your encouragement and positive reinforcement. All of the work on the chapters and endless typing and editing was all done with a big smile, as of an angel. Thanks, I love you.

Table of Contents

Preface

In writing this book, I hope to do three things: repay a kindness, inspire hope and confidence, and close out a chapter of my life.

The first kindness was God's, who put a series of remarkable people in my path exactly when I needed them. Their kindness and compassion have made it possible for me to reach this point on my journey from darkness into light and enabled me to look back without fear or anger to write this book.

In writing I, Witness, I also wish to inspire others who have found themselves trapped within the coils of any group that seeks to control or demean them. The message is simple: You are meant to own your own soul and no one other than God, Himself, has any claim upon it. No one else has the right to dictate your faith or set your spiritual value.

On the other side of this message is responsibility, of course. If we are the owners of our souls, then it is our responsibility to care for them, to educate them, to clothe them in fitting garments. In a word—virtues.

This is not something we should let anyone else do for us. We must have faith that, as Christ Jesus said, what we earnestly seek we will find:

Ask, and it will be given to you; seek, and you will find; knock, and it will be opened to you. For everyone who asks receives, and he who seeks finds, and to him who knocks it will be opened. Or what man is there among you who, if his son asks for bread, will give him a stone? Or if he asks for a fish, will he give him a serpent? If you then, being evil, know how to give good gifts to your children, how much more will your Father who is in heaven give good things to those who ask Him! Therefore, whatever you want men to do to you, do also to them, for this is the Law and the Prophets.

—Matthew 7:7-12, (NKJ)

So, there it is: a promise and a responsibility. A covenant between each of us and our Divine Parent. It is in the spirit of honoring this covenant that I offer this book and suggest to each reader that your soul is your own—a gift from a loving God.

I, Witness is the record of my journey through the valleys of uncertainty, fear, and guilt to the green pastures of Psalm. It chronicles my steps from a closed society out into the open sunlight, and shuts the gate on the shadows I've left behind. I pray that those who read it may see that they, too, can find a path to a fuller, freer life of faith.

—The Author

I

The End Times

Worlds shatter in strange ways.

Sometimes it's the result of an act of violence, or of unbearable cruelty, or even of kindness. The act is committed and a fault line rips through the core of your existence. The world comes apart beneath your feet.

But what "rocked" my world on a sunny Saturday morning in the spring of 1999 was a simple question: "Dan, do you know what you're going to say at the door today?"

My wife, Andrea, and I were riding that morning in the back seat of the Presiding Congregation Elder's car, preparing to spread some "good news about Jehovah's Kingdom" to the people living in this beautiful, orderly neighborhood. I looked at Andrea and realized I hadn't a clue. I'd been sitting in the back of the car for some time, staring at the latest issues of the *Watchtower* and *Awake!*, but I had no idea what I was going to say.

"Not yet," I admitted and quickly flipped through the magazines looking for introductory ideas that might arouse interest in the people we visited. The "issues" that day were: The Signs of the Times of the End (meaning food shortages, earthquakes, sickness, death, war) and Raising Your Family In This Day and Age.

Glancing down at the tracts, my eyes snagged on a familiar Bible prophecy. It painted a rosy picture of what life would be like when "those hoping in Jehovah are the ones that will possess the earth" (Psalm 37:9). Skipping down, I read: "...and soon, the blind will see, the lame will walk, there will be no more death or pain. The world will be a paradise... We must turn from our wicked ways, for the whole world is lying in the power of the wicked one, Satan the devil. For the Bible clearly warns us that 'a little while longer...and the wicked will be no more.'"

The "wicked," of course, were those living outside of the Jehovah's Witness organization—the Watchtower Bible and Tract Society. The people I was on my way to visit were all part of Satan's world no matter what religion they followed or with what devotion they worshipped. Not even those who thought of themselves as faithful Christians would be spared Jehovah's wrath. They were scheduled for destruction.

"We are seeing living proof today that the end will soon come," the magazine said. That proof was in the wars and "rumors of wars," the rise of nation against nation, natural disasters such as earthquakes and food shortages. Tribulation was everywhere and false prophets arose by the dozen to offer solutions. But the only solution was in my hands: "And this good news of the kingdom will be preached in all the inhabited earth for a witness to all the nations; and then the end will come." (Matthew 24:14)

My eyes blurred. This wasn't "good news." This was negative! Hurtful. Polarizing. *Terrifying.* These people didn't want to hear this stuff. Why would they? They had their gleaming new cars, their happy-go-lucky children, their nice, neat homes, their fine clothes—they even seemed emotionally happy and whole! They had peace. It was as if *they* were the blessed ones.

Why would they listen to me? I thought. It just didn't make sense.

There was only one truth I was certain of in that moment: No one wanted to hear about the coming End with its judgment, destruction, and death. No one wanted to know a God who would visit them with cataclysmic war and sickness. No one wanted to believe in a God who would commit wholesale massacre of even those who professed to love and believe in Him. No one living in these lovely homes would embrace my view of what was going on all around them—why should they?

I was filled with sudden loathing. Turning to my wife I mumbled, "I can't give people this crap." Before I could consider my actions, I had thrown the *Watchtower* and *Awake!* magazines to the floor of the car.

Andrea's face reflected this sudden and incomprehensible act as vividly as any mirror. In her stark expression of horror I saw myself as a babbling wild man, stripped of rational thought, speaking the unspeakable.

I descended into chaos. What on earth was I thinking? I'd just thrown away Jehovah's spiritual food—food offered by the "faithful and discreet slave," God's visible organization on earth today, the Watchtower Society.

Oh God, HELP ME! I thought. *What am I doing?*

I glanced up at the Elder behind the wheel of the car who was chatting with the brother in the passenger seat. He hadn't heard my outburst, but even now he was pulling the car into the curb along a sunny, tree-lined street. I gathered up the discarded magazines with shaking hands and herded my chaotic thoughts into strict obedience. Tucking the *Watchtower* and *Awake!* under my arm, I gave Andrea a reassuring smile.

I'm fine.

Moments later we were knocking at someone's door. I listened to Andrea asking questions about what they thought the future held. I pretended interest in their answers, all the while quivering in sick dread. When Andrea looked to me for input, I opened my lips and spoke from the well of information in my head. But my heart lay frozen in my breast.

What had just happened to me?

This bewildering episode started a cascade of events— events I now see as Divine synchronicity—God's perfect timing. The questions I had been afraid to ask within my own mind and heart, the truth I had been loathe to find, the dysfunctionality of the organization that had steered my life—all of this was only now beginning to dawn on my mind. But there was an unstoppable urge in my soul to demand answers to those questions, to find that truth, to see what I had not wanted to see during my lifetime as a Jehovah's Witness.

I had the overpowering sense that I was losing control of the person I thought I was. It was as if I had stepped out of a fog into clear daylight or awakened from a long, drugged sleep.

What's going on? I begged of myself and God. *Am I going crazy? Am I having a nervous breakdown?*

But I would soon be moved to ask myself how I could *not*

have asked those questions. How I could *not* have sought that truth. How I could *not* have seen what had been going on around me for forty years.

"In a moment," the Apostle Peter says in his first letter to the Corinthians (15:52), "in the twinkling of an eye…we shall be changed."

In that moment, I was changed irrevocably. I had stepped over a line and could not go back.

II

A Family in the Fold

The Day is Drawing Near

I grew up with the notion that "the day is drawing near"—the day, that is, for the End of the World. So had my mother, her siblings, and their mother and father. Even *my* father—the son of a Pentecostal minister—had lived with it from the moment he determined to marry a Jehovah's Witness.

And so had every generation of Jehovah's Witnesses before them.

Because this world will soon end, the reasoning went, Jehovah's Witnesses should not seek to take part in it. That included such seemingly innocent things as observing birthdays or holidays, accepting awards, or taking part in activities that did not contribute directly to the "health" of the Kingdom Hall.

It also included things most people in our common culture think of as necessities. Why learn to drive if you'll never need to own a car, or seek a higher education if you won't live long enough to use it? Why strive for career advancement or follow a heartfelt calling when it will only distract you from the Lord's work? Indeed, why even concern yourself with your physical health if God is going to restore or recreate your body?

The only necessary vehicle, the only needed education, the only true medicine, were contained in the pages of the Watchtower publications.

Jehovah's Witnesses knew what the future held, and they anticipated it the way my childhood friends anticipated Christmas morning. And why not? It would be a wonderful future...for them.

SOON! AN END TO DISABILITIES! trumpets an article on the Watchtower website. But this miracle will not be caused by breakthroughs in medicine. It will occur because *very soon* the world will end, and people with disabilities will be given perfect bodies...and perfect minds. Of course, this is only true of those who are Jehovah's Witnesses in "good standing" at the time of the End. But it is an amazing promise, nonetheless. It meant my father would one day be healthy, energetic, and free of gout, my mother whole, my aunt no longer "mongoloid."

It's a promise that captures the imagination, engages the emotions, offers hope to the hopeless. And certainly there was no one more in need of hope than my mother, Sheryl Mae Clark.

The oldest of six children born to the Hopewell family, Mom was raised in the Kingdom Hall and had never known life apart from it. While I know the names of her siblings—Beth, Warren, Greg, Nick, and Janice (who had Down Syndrome)— her parents were always just Grandma and Grandpa Hopewell. I eventually discovered my grandfather's first name was Henry, but Grandma remains nameless. My father's parents were Ron and Mary—something I learned by going through an old family photo album—and he had an older brother, Arthur. We were not a close-knit family.

Nor were we "landed." Despite the fact that Garden City, Michigan had been planned as a so-called "garden community" with houses built on lots of up to an acre (to encourage small-scale farming), my family lived in a two-bedroom, one-bathroom bungalow—all my father could afford on his earnings as a road construction worker.

Until I was in my late teens, most of Dad's work was out-of-state. His job was to cut a line down the middle of the road with a diamond blade saw, through solid concrete. He did this for eight to ten hours a day without earplugs or headphones—at the cost of his hearing. He was regularly gone for two week periods and home for two days during the construction season. During these absences, we would be left alone with Mom.

Paranoid schizophrenia was my mother's personal form of hopelessness. I don't know when she was diagnosed with the disease, but I can't remember a time when she was free of it. I knew her as a slovenly, overweight woman (four-foot-eleven and weighing in excess of 200 pounds) who cared very little for her physical appearance or cleanliness, except for a peculiar fixation with fingernail polish.

But I had seen the photograph of Sheryl and Del Clark on their wedding day. It showed an attractive young woman who could not have weighed more than ninety-seven pounds, and a well-built, robust young man. But the Del Clark I knew never weighed less than 300 pounds and seemed to gain weight and weariness with every seasonal layoff.

No one in Mom's family fully understood what had

happened to her. Family members have commented that she seemed a perfectly normal young girl up until she was about nineteen. Of course normal, in my mother's case, meant she had been removed from school in her early teens to "help out" at home and be the primary caregiver for her siblings, including her disabled little sister. It meant she lived in fear of an abusive father about whom even us boys were warned, "Don't sit in Grandpa's lap." Of her mental disorder, her brother Nick would only say that one day she crossed the street to the school grounds where she met "someone" and simply came back *changed*.

Mom's condition made it impossible for her to function normally. She wouldn't or couldn't do housework or shop, so the chores fell to the male members of the household. But the physical debilities that came with Dad's obesity limited his contribution even when he was at home, and few young boys are good at housework; the Clark house was in a constant state of chaotic filth.

The thing I remember most clearly (other than the challenge of bunking with my brothers Keith, Don, and Peter in one tiny bedroom) was the foul odor of the house. It came by this reek naturally, because the tub was usually filled with the dirty clothes of four growing boys. Taking a shower required that you remove these items from the tub. This was a task that gave even a rough-and-tumble bunch like us pause; the fabric was permeated with molds, mildews, and critters that like cozy, moist places.

Entering the kitchen was as much a challenge as bathing. For one thing it required that you play hopscotch with the puddles of pee left by one or more of our mutts. The kitchen floor was ruined eventually, and the tiles were warped and uneven because of the damage to the sub-flooring. This room, too, had its own unique aroma—dog urine and rotting food. There were dirty dishes everywhere that did not get washed if we boys didn't wash them. In the living room, the dogs' fleas were so thick you could see them leaping out of the carpet. My brother Keith had an allergy to flea bites and scratched himself raw.

This is not to say that Dad did nothing around the house. He made a gallant effort one winter to remove and rebuild the kitchen cabinets. Unhappily, he never completed the project and they went unfinished and without hardware for as long as I lived in the house.

And, of course, when Dad was home he was responsible for Mom.

He displayed his mastery of Mom by yelling at her repeatedly to "Get up, woman!" whenever he wanted food or drink. He would issue this order either from the sofa, where he normally slept, or from the floor next to the sofa where he often ended up when the pad beneath him would slip under his weight, dumping him there during the night.

Mom would not get up, and Dad would yell at one of us next, "Get me the pellet gun, boy!" Then he would pump up the air gun, roll his great bulk to where he could sight down the hallway (it was too much effort to stand), and fire into the bedroom, hitting the headboard above Mom's head.

"Stop it, Del!" she'd shriek. "You're going to hit me with one of those things and put my eye out!"

He never did hit her, much less put her eye out, but he did put many tiny dents in the wall and headboard and shatter their dresser mirror with a bad ricochet. The mirror never got fixed.

Eventually Mom would give in, get up, and come into the

living room where she would punch Dad in the arm and say, "You could have hurt me, Del. What the hell were you doing?"

And then, just when we thought a fight was about to break out, she'd smile winsomely, snuggle up beside him on the sofa, and give him a hug.

Grown-ups, we'd think. *Can't live with 'em...*

I don't mean to imply that we Clark boys were earnest little angels who took care of their Mommy without complaint. We complained plenty. We swore. We yelled. We gnashed our teeth. Keith had an especially smart mouth and spent much of his boyhood in trouble for it.

"I'm going to tell your father," Mom would threaten, and we'd repent and promise to do whatever she asked if only she wouldn't tell Dad. She always accepted the deal.

We bought her endless bottles of fingernail polish; we did chores, washed clothes and dishes, gave the dog flea baths. But when Dad would come home, she'd tell him every niggling detail about our disobedience and sassy mouths.

Every time. And every time we were surprised by the seeming betrayal. You'd think we'd have learned, especially since these disclosures of our infamy were always followed by Dad knocking us around a bit.

"You'd better listen to your mom, boys!" he'd say, punctuating the words with well-aimed blows. His abuse had a pattern: he would punch you in the arms—first one side, then the other—until you fell over, then kick you in the butt or leg, shouting, "Get out of my sight, boy!"

Mom played cheerleader. "That's what he deserves, Del," she'd tell him as he delivered our punishment. And to us she'd simply say, "Don't you ever do that again."

Inside Sheryl Clark

Mom needed Dad. She needed him in a way that left her vulnerable and uncertain, which only worsened her already precarious mental and emotional state. She was a virtual prisoner in her own home, bound by her mood disorder, her slovenliness, her weight, and her lack of ability to drive.

It was an inevitable fact of life that every three years or so, Mom's medications would fail, her hopelessness would overwhelm her, and she'd have a complete breakdown. These breakdowns were almost always triggered by her fears that Dad someday would fail to come home.

One day, a day or so before Dad was due to return from his usual rotation with the highway crew, I walked into the kitchen to find Mom sitting at the table, bent over, her filthy, unkempt hair hanging limply in her face. She had on the same dress she'd worn for weeks and the kitchen reeked of her vinegreg body odor.

"Dad's not coming home," she told me.

She sounded so certain I was thrown into immediate turmoil. I fell to my knees in front of her and begged her to take it back. "Mom, no! Don't say that. He's coming home! He *is*."

She began to sob uncontrollably. "No, never, Danny. He's *never* coming home! And it's my fault. It's because I'm sick. Because I've got mental problems. That's why he's left me."

She felt unsafe, she told me—in her own house, on our quiet street. She was scared. And looking into her eyes, I was scared too.

"Dan, can you make me feel safe?" she pleaded.

Could I? I didn't know. I only knew I was willing to do *anything* for her. "What do you want me to do?" I asked.

She had me put three-inch screws in every window in the house so that they wouldn't open. She also had me nail the back door shut.

I had no idea what she was afraid of.

Paranoia. That was invariably the prelude to a full scale break with reality. The next stage was storytelling—starting with fairly believable stories about when she was growing up. This always led to tales about Dad and who he had flirted with while they were dating (or at least who she *thought* he'd flirted with). She'd then move into the next stage: becoming consumed with what family and friends were thinking about her.

"Do you think so-and-so thinks I'm crazy?" she'd ask me, as if I had any reason to know.

If she happened to be in a social situation (a rare occurrence) and anyone said anything to her that hinted she was less than perfectly sane, she would come home terrified.

"So-and-so told me I didn't make any sense," she'd say, then go off into a fugue of self-doubt, certain that her friends all thought her mad.

I'm sure many of them did. I can only hope that most of them understood that she had no control over her illness—an illness that even today is only dimly understood.

In her last stages of crumbling, Mom's fears gave birth to wilder, more implausible stories. She delivered these to the neighbors—in person and in great detail. And so we'd get the inevitable phone call telling us that Mom had reached a breaking point.

"Your mother is running down the street naked," they'd tell us, their voices heavy with pity and embarrassment, and we'd find her discarded dress somewhere in the house, usually near the door through which she'd made her escape.

It was always my brother Keith who would bring her home, sobbing and telling crazy, made-up stories that I can only imagine must have been the product of hallucinations—sights only she could see, voices only she could hear. And it was Keith who would somehow manage to get her to the hospital. She didn't want to go. Hospitals were evil. They did bad things to you there. The staff couldn't be trusted—not the doctors, not the nurses, not the helpful, smiling volunteers. They each had their own agendas—their own reasons for treating you, for holding you, for offering you clothes, food, and medication. None of those reasons were good.

So, Mom always fought Keith, and he would doggedly, patiently take her to the Eloise Hospital in neighboring Inkster. Then we would call Dad at his hotel and leave a message telling him to please come home—Mom had broken down.

He never failed to return. And he got there as quickly as was physically possible, sometimes driving eight to ten hours straight to reach us.

A Visit to Hell

I was ten the first time I visited Eloise Hospital with my father. I knew nothing about this sort of place; it was not something a ten-year-old child should be able to imagine. Dad tried to prepare me for it in his own way, but of that conversation, I remember only that he said, "Your mother's on the eighth floor." The words and the heavy, flat tone of his voice left me with the conviction that the higher up in the building a person was, the sicker they were.

"We may or may not get in today," he added, "depending on how your mom's feeling."

In other words, depending upon how sane she was that day.

We arrived at the hospital around 10:00 a.m. The building, located in the poorest section of Inkster, was dated, dark, and dingy. Its façade was of tired, stained brick, its poverty written on it as if in loud, invisible graffiti left by some spiritual vandal. We stood on the sidewalk outside and looked up at the eighth floor. There were bars on every window. It was a prison. It was a zoo.

We went in to meet the inmates—the wild animals.

On the floor that contained my mother, my father led me to an immensely tall steel door and knocked on it. I stared up at the door wondering what was so dangerous that it required this sort of armor plating to hold it in. My mother wasn't dangerous, yet she was behind this door.

No one answered Dad's knock. I saw a large button to the left of the door and pointed at it.

"Go ahead," Dad said. "Push it."

I did. It set off a buzzer so loud I jumped and covered my ears. The harsh, metallic screech drew someone to the door. Its opening was as impressive as its size. It sounded the way I imagined a castle drawbridge would—metal scraping and clanging on metal.

I suppose I expected to see a knight or a dragon awaiting us in the hallway beyond. There was neither. A female nurse stood on the other side of the door, her expression stern, frank—closer to a dragon than a knight.

She ushered us into Hell.

The odor that came through that door was a sickly combination of disinfectant, human body odor, and disease. Overlaying it was a scent like burnt flesh. Dirty sunlight cascaded into the long hallway from rows of windows; they were filthy and striped by the bars we had glimpsed from the sidewalk.

"We're here to see Sheryl Clark," Dad said, and we began our journey down the hall in the nurse's wake.

The floors we shuffled over (why does such a place reduce all visitors to shuffling?) were as dated as the exterior of the building—flyspeck stick-on tile. The People of the Hallway seemed like the living dead, arisen from some movie-set grave-yard to haunt the corridors of Eloise Hospital. I shrank from them in fear and wondered if I would scream.

It was the nurse who screamed. "Sheryl! You have guests!"

Her shrill cry caused several of the Zombies to break off from their meanders and approach us. "We'll help you find Sheryl," they mumbled.

We kept moving—past the Zombies, past the woman who repeatedly pounded her bandaged, bleeding foot against the floor—and finally turned a corner into a large, sunny, high-ceilinged room filled with orderly rows of tables.

And there was Mom, sitting alone, head drooping, hair oily, dirty, and uncombed. Her stained dress seemed two sizes too small. She was looking down at her fingernails and exam-ining them as if checking her nail polish, but they were bare and bitten to the quick.

She looked up at us and asked, "You didn't tell anyone I'm in here did you?"

"No," Dad replied, and I shook my head.

In a voice slurred by tranquillizers, she asked if we'd come to take her home.

My heart broke. This was my sweet, lovable, vulnerable mother. Of course I wanted to take her home. But this was also the woman who could turn, in the blink of an eye, into a spiteful stranger you were sure could kill you with her bare hands.

As we visited with Mom, other patients came up to talk to us. Mom guarded us jealously—clenching her fists and threatening her fellow patients with violence. Alone with us she told horror stories of things she claimed happened in the solitary confinement of the Rubber Room. They made her eat off the floor, she said, and would slide her food through her own urine, contaminating it. They used sexual abuse as a tool to force her to comply with their directions, and she confided in a whisper that many of the female inmates were lesbians who tried to crawl into bed with her.

When she was out on the ward, as she was this day, there were other dangers. Patting her outworn dress, she told Dad, "Don't bother to bring me good clothes, Del. They'll be stolen the first day."

At ten, I had no concept of either sexual abuse or lesbianism, but I understood theft. Who would want to steal Mom's clothing? Even her best was threadbare and ill-fitting. Looking back as an adult, I can only wonder what effect these stories had on my father.

At the end of our visit, as Dad rose to leave, Mom cried, "Why am I sick, Del? Why do I have mental problems?"

Dad had no answer to that, nor did I. Nor did any of the trained medical professionals who worked at Eloise. But if the teachings of the Watchtower Society were to be believed, it didn't matter. It would all be over soon, for all of us. People in God's Kingdom on Earth wouldn't have paranoid schizophrenia.

SOON! AN END TO DISABILITIES—yes, but how soon? Soon enough for my mother?

"Take me home, Del!" she pleaded. "This is Hell."

When Dad could only hug her and offer weak consolation,

she looked to me. "Dan," she said, "will you take me out of here? This coward—your father—*won't*."

In the end I could do no more than my father had done—hug her, hold her, just for a moment. And one other thing: I could cry with her, because we both knew she wasn't leaving this place any time soon.

As we retraced our steps through the Hall of the Undead, I could hear Mom crying in the big, sunny room—confused, hopeless, imprisoned.

I looked up at my silent father and wondered, *How do we just leave? How do we leave Mom to be abused, beaten, and straight-jacketed—or to imagine that these things have happened to her? How do we leave her so empty and alone?*

I didn't ask this aloud. In fact, Dad and I didn't say another word to each other for the rest of the day, as if speaking of it would somehow make things worse.

Growing up I often wondered if there were anything I could have done to keep her out of Eloise. I suppose my father must have wondered the same thing as he walked the hospital ward, or as he answered the inevitable phone call that brought him home to his broken wife and frightened children.

Perhaps there is a miracle in that—that he always *did* come home.

A Father, Failed

In many ways Del Clark was a "stand-up guy." He performed a physically tasking job in order to put food on the table. He did always come home to us. And he tried to give us some sort of spiritual education within the Kingdom Hall of Jehovah's Witnesses.

Unlike his wife, Del Clark did not grow up in the Watchtower

Society. He was raised in a Pentecostal home by a mother who was pastor of her own church. His father, Ron, had no love for organized religion, but he took care of his wife's church building and kept the grass green and mowed. I remember Grandpa Clark as a jokester—a man who loved laughter.

Grandma Clark, on the other hand, had little sense of humor, especially when it came to the woman her son had chosen to marry. Nor was she one to pull punches. She let it be known from day one that marrying Sheryl Hopewell had ruined her boy, leading him to join a "cult."

This did not cause her to disown Dad, however. Mary and Ron Clark were well-off enough financially to allow them to purchase a new car every two or three years. They always bought two-door coupes, and they always gave the old one to Dad. He loved those cars. They allowed him to push the driver's seat way back and recline it, the easier to get his 400-pound bulk behind the wheel.

When Dad was home, we would all pile into his car to attend meetings at the Kingdom Hall. It seems odd, looking back on it—Mom was the lifetime Jehovah's Witness and Dad a late convert, yet he was the one who always made the effort to get us to meetings, to hold Bible and Watchtower studies in our home, to keep us in the faith community. Mom followed along with a smile, but it was Dad's job as head of the household to rally the troops. Naturally, he could only do this when he was home, so our attendance at meetings was sporadic. When Dad was at work, we simply didn't go.

Meeting days were not pleasant for us boys. Kids never like to be dragged away from play to go to a sit-down-and-shut-up event, but our aversion went beyond that. Dad was always angry when we went to the Kingdom Hall. I'm not sure why.

Perhaps he was angry with us kids for whining and grousing about having to go; perhaps he was angry at having to flog us into going; perhaps he was angry at Mom for not getting us to the meetings in his absence and so drawing the quiet censure of the Elders.

In any event, he would inevitably holler us to the door, pausing at the last moment to pull his sweater out from under the sofa, wrinkled and covered with German Shepherd hair. Mom's dresses were equally disheveled, and the entire family was unkempt and smelly. I've no doubt this caused my father considerable shame. We always arrived a little late and sat at the very back of the Hall where we were less likely to be noticed by other members...and from which point we could beat a hasty retreat.

Dad's shame extended to more than just our poor physical presentation, however. A more critical failure was his inability to educate us in the spiritual work we were expected to do. He wasn't home to lead our family, as befits a strong head-of-household. He was off working at something other than the Lord's business in these "last days" before the end of the world. As a result of our less-than-regular attendance, our lack of home study sessions, our spiritual poverty, we Clark boys were never ready for the Question and Answer portion of the meeting, nor did we join in the door-to-door ministry.

Perhaps what I took for anger in Dad was guilt and shame...and fear that he was failing not just his family and congregation, but God, Himself. In a society that scrupulously tracks both attendance and Field Service (door-to-door) hours, Del Clark's family was a disappointment. The Clarks were "weak," in need of extra encouragement, a family the Elders took special pains to greet on meeting days.

But only on meeting days.

Because we were "weak," other members avoided association with us outside of the Kingdom Hall. Jehovah's spirit was not with us, and we would most likely not be "concealed in the day of Jehovah's anger."

All of this sat heavily upon the stooped shoulders of Delvin Clark, and on meeting days, he could only sit and stew in his shame, listening to the exhortations from the podium, believing that he had failed.

But he had not failed. What failed were the prophetic interpretations of the Watchtower Bible and Tract Society, given and retracted, reshaped and reissued over a period of 136 years.

As I write this book, my father is dead and my mother still lives within the solid and very real walls of Hell.

The End did not come soon enough for either of them.

III

Witnesses of the Kingdom

An Angry God

*"...before there comes upon you people **the burning anger of Jehovah**, before there comes upon you **the day of Jehovah's anger**, seek Jehovah, all you meek ones of the earth, who have practiced His own judicial decision. Seek righteousness, seek meekness. Probably you may be concealed **in the day of Jehovah's anger**."*
— Zephaniah 2:2-3 (emphasis mine)

This verse, quoted from the World Bible and Tract Society's New World Translation of the Bible, is at the heart of Watchtower theology. It begs the question: *Why is Jehovah angry?*

The short answer is: because of the sin of Adam and Eve. The original pair are believed to have been encouraged by Satan to eat of a literal "Tree of the Knowledge of Good and

Evil," which caused them to become aware that there *were* such things as good and evil.

They also became self-conscious. But it's neither the discovery of good and evil nor of our own humanity that has been the focus of church doctrine for so many centuries. It's the shame of the "original sin" that made Adam and Eve unable to carry out God's purpose—to fill the earth with "righteous families."

Jehovah's universal sovereignty is at stake. With His original purpose thwarted, God had to make alternate plans. Those plans call for this world to end in horrific destruction and for a new one to be raised from its ashes. It is belief and *hope* in this plan that drive the activities of the Kingdom Hall.

What's hopeful about the destruction of the world? The belief among Jehovah's Witnesses is that this destruction is not total, but rather that "…Jehovah created the earth to be the Paradise home of the human family." (*Watchtower,* November 2003)

This belief has been at the core of Watchtower teaching since its birth in the mid-to-late 1800s, and it has dictated the way in which the WTS interprets scripture.

In the early-to-mid 1800s, events in the world—especially in Palestine—led many Biblical scholars to believe that the "time of the end" was near. The Jews were no longer barred from returning to the Holy Land; the Gospel had been preached to every "corner" of the globe. These seeming fulfillments of Biblical prophecy combined with time-related prophecies in the Old Testament book of Daniel raised the expectation that Christ would return some time in 1844. The fact that this millennial zeal was being felt around the world in non-Christian religions probably contributed to the excitement.

A number of millennial movements arose worldwide at

this time, but of those born in the United States only Seventh Day Adventism, the Church of Latter Day Saints (Mormons), and the Watchtower Society still exist in any great numbers.

When 1844 passed and Christ had not returned as expected, this period of history became known as "The Great Disappointment." William Miller, the Bible scholar at the center of the millennial storm in America, died in 1849, still hopeful that Christ's return was near. Others began to re-calculate, trying to settle on a new date for the end of the world. The Seventh Day Adventists, for example, decided that Christ had entered the "sanctuary" in Heaven in 1844 to begin judging humanity and would return when that judgement was complete.

Meanwhile, in Allegheny, Pennsylvania, evangelist Charles Taze Russell joined with two other millennial preachers to start a group called simply "Bible Students." It was from this group that the Watchtower Bible and Tract Society grew.

The WTS rejected quite a bit of what has become mainstream Christian doctrine: the Trinity, the belief that Christ *is* God in a material sense, and the immortality of the human soul to name but a few. They rejected the celebration of Christmas, citing it as a pagan tradition, and deplored the celebration of birthdays. They did, however, teach that Christ's death was sacrificial, that He paid the ransom for the sin brought into the world by Adam and Eve's rebellion, and that He had arisen from death as a "spirit person."

And of course they taught that He would return and crush the earthly kingdoms, paving the way for the Kingdom of God. This belief—that we were living in the scriptural "time of the end"—continued to drive the group's teachings even after the Great Disappointment. God would soon destroy the world and all its sinful inhabitants and bequeath it as an eternal paradise to His faithful servants.

This key teaching has shaped the reality of the Kingdom Hall and the lives of its members *for over 130 years.*

You see, Jehovah's Witnesses believe that Paradise is a physical place where "...under the rule of Jesus Christ and his heavenly co-rulers, peace and happiness will prevail in all the earth. Those in God's memory will be resurrected and will enjoy perfect health. By their faithfulness to God, obedient mankind will be granted what our original parents lost—everlasting life in human perfection on a paradise earth." (*Watchtower,* November 2003) By "heavenly co-rulers" is meant the 144,000 "anointed remnant" spoken of in the Revelation of Saint John. According to the WTS interpretation of this scripture these are the only souls who will actually spend eternity in heaven and be allowed to "partake of the emblems" (receive communion).

When Jehovah vents His mighty wrath He will not literally destroy the planet, but He will destroy "the world" created by the evil people living on it. Evil people are, quite simply, those who are not Jehovah's Witnesses in "good standing." Everyone else will be utterly destroyed, no matter how sincere their love of God or their belief in Him, how pure and devoted their lives, or how loving their hearts.

This expectation is based on a passage in the New Testament book of Matthew:

...if the householder had known in what watch the thief was coming, he would have kept awake and not allowed his house to be broken into. On this account you too prove yourselves ready, because at an hour that you do not think to be it, the Son of man

*is coming. **Who really is the faithful and discreet slave whom his master appointed over his domestics, to give them their food at the proper time?** Happy is that slave if his master on arriving finds him doing so. Truly I say to you, He will appoint him over all his belongings.*

—Jesus, Matthew 24:43-47 (emphasis mine)

This verse, with its stress on the readiness of the "faithful and discreet slave" and on his being found doing his duty upon his master's return is why door-to-door missionary work is so important to the Kingdom Hall. The world is a ticking time bomb. To do anything with your life but study scripture and spread the faith is a sinful waste of precious time.

I'm reminded of a recent conversation I had with my brother Keith about this. He had been offered a wonderful job with opportunities for career growth, better pay, and interesting work. He turned it down. When I asked him why, he told me, "The Watchtower has released some new litera-ture, Dan. Something's about to happen. It could be any day now. Why should I invest time and energy in my work? Do you think I'm going to give up a place in Paradise for a good job in this world?"

He continued to muddle along in his old job, struggling to keep his multiple sclerosis under control, so that he could spend more time in Field Service. If he was out teaching door-to-door when the end came, he was assured of a place in Paradise.

Get Out from Among Them

Lack of participation in "the world" is an important element of Jehovah's Witness belief. For many years, church members were not permitted to vote in secular elections, a teaching that resulted in persecution and imprisonment in some countries (Germany and the Cameroons, for example). The December 1973 *Watchtower* magazine said of Jehovah's Witnesses that, "They do not run for political offices, or vote for political candidates." Joining secular or quasi-religious organizations was also forbidden. To join the YMCA, according to the January 1, 1979 issue of *Watchtower* "would amount to apostasy." (By 1999 the position on voting had softened somewhat, leaving it to the conscience of the individual believer.)

Naturally the organization models this unworldly behavior to its membership by not participating in other organizations' efforts toward what may seem like common human goals. For example, the United Nations, with its charter of global justice and maintaining international peace and security, might seem like a fulfillment of that well-known prophecy in the Book of Isaiah that the nations will "beat their swords into plowshares and their spears into pruning hooks." In fact, there's a statue in the United Nations Garden that bears the legend "Let Us Beat Swords into Plowshares." But the Watchtower Society takes a dim view of both the UN and its predecessor, the League of Nations.

The WTS has referred to the United Nations as a "disgusting thing" and "a blasphemous counterfeit of God's Messianic Kingdom." It has associated the UN with the "scarlet-colored wild beast…full of blasphemous names" spoken of in the Book of Revelation. A book entitled *Revelation: Its Grand Climax at Hand* states that "…men have set up this *multinational idol* as a substitute for God's Kingdom—to accomplish what God says his Kingdom alone can accomplish." (emphasis mine)

"Babylonish religion, particularly Christendom," *Revelation* continues, "has linked itself with the League of Nations and its successor (the United Nations)." And as to anyone supporting the United Nations, the Watchtower Society states plainly that "The UN's founders and admirers do not have their names recorded in God's scroll of life." In 1963, Jehovah's Witnesses the world over codified this doctrine by issuing a convention resolution against the United Nations.

There is another more notorious way in which Jehovah's Witnesses separate themselves from the world—their historical refusal to accept blood transfusions. This has been an important doctrine at least since the July 1, 1945 *Watchtower* denounced blood transfusions as "pagan" and "God -dishonoring." In 1961, *The Watchtower* cited blood transfusion as a reason for disfellowshipping (being removed from the roles of Jehovah's Witnesses), stating categorically: "Whether whole or fractional, *one's own or someone else's*, transfused or injected, it is wrong." (emphasis mine)

So important is this principle that Jehovah's Witnesses have traditionally carried Hospital Care Cards that refuse blood transfusions. These are legal documents signed by the individual member and two Elders that are binding upon medical attendants under threat of lawsuit. The WTS also appoints specially trained Blood Liaisons to intercede for Jehovah's Witnesses who are hospitalized and in jeopardy of being transfused. These Blood Liaisons are also dispatched when a pregnant Jehovah's Witness goes into labor.

The doctrine is based on a number of passages in the Bible that condemn the "eating" of blood which is believed to contain the soul of the animal or person:

> *Genesis 9:4* – *"But flesh (meat) with...blood...ye shall not eat."*
> *Leviticus 17:12-14* – *"...No soul of you shall eat blood ...whosoever eateth it shall be cut off."*
> *Acts 15:29* – *"That ye abstain...from blood..."*
> *Acts 21:25* – *"...Gentiles...keep themselves from things offered to idols and from blood..."*

While others interpret these passages as dietary laws, the Watchtower Society has gone so far as to urge believers to "discontinue their chemotherapy treatments when platelet transfusions are needed." (*Jehovah's Witnesses: Witness Position on Therapy*, Official Watchtower website).

Naturally, horror stories about transfusions abound. In addition to fears that they spread AIDS, hepatitis, and other diseases, Watchtower literature has added a few more worries. Quoting a Dr. Americo Valerio *Watchtower* tells us, "Moral insanity, sexual perversions, repression, inferiority complexes, petty crimes—these often follow in the wake of a blood transfusion." How? According to the book *Who is Your Doctor and Why*, "The blood in any person is in reality the person himself. It contains all the peculiarities of the individual..."

This doctrine has had a profound impact on individuals and families within the Kingdom Hall. People have died in the absence of transfusions, families have been torn apart over the acceptance or rejection of the procedure, members have been disfellowshipped for acting against the official WTS position—a position that was to have an unexpected impact on my own life.

Prove Yourselves Ready

As I said earlier, 1844 was the first date that a significant group of Bible scholars from around the world agreed Christ would return. When 1844 passed without a worldwide cataclysm, it required resetting the clock. Charles Taze Russell reset his organization's clock to 1874. When that year also passed without Divine intervention, the leaders of the WTS did two things: they reset the date yet again and recast the significance of the date that had just passed. This became the pattern for years to come. (See **Table 1: A Timeline of Some WTS Prophecy** at the end of this chapter.)

The most significant of these prophecies in my life were the ones related to the year 1914. This was the year in which, according to the Watchtower Society, Christ began His rule in heaven. It became the focus of End Times prophecy because of what Jesus said when His disciples asked what would be the signs of His coming at the end of the age. He replied in part, *"You are going to hear of wars and reports of wars; see that you are not terrified. For these things must take place, but the end is not yet."* (Matthew 24:6) Later in this dialogue, after describing the coming tribulations, He adds, *"Truly I say to you that this generation will by no means pass away until all these things occur."* (Matthew 24:34)

From this the WTS determined that 1914, with its Great War, marked the beginning of the signs of the end. They took Jesus' words about "this generation" to apply to the generation alive in 1914. Therefore, the end *must come* before the generation alive in 1914 was gone. Defining "generation" to mean the length of a human life, the Watchtower Society figured that a generation was between seventy and eighty years. The math was simple: adding 70 or 80 to 1914 yielded a range between 1984 and 1994. Even if you calculated a generation of ninety years, 2004 would be an outside date.

Despite its own words of warning about "fixing dates," as late as May 1992 *The Watchtower* proclaimed, "Today, a small percentage of mankind can still recall the dramatic events of 1914. Will that elderly generation pass away before God saves the earth from ruin? Not according to Bible prophecy."

This was taught to all Jehovah's Witnesses of my generation with great certainty and well-documented in the book we trained with: the so-called "Paradise Book" (*You Can Live Forever in Paradise*). But as the last of "that generation" passed away, and the millennium went by without any real calamity, the organization went into another period of reassessment. Some tracts and books were taken out of circulation, others were edited or replaced.

Two examples of this are the "Paradise Book" itself, which is no longer in print, and *Why Awake! is Published,* which has been edited to omit references to the 1914 "generation prophecy." Prior to November of 1995 the tract read: "Most important, this magazine builds confidence in the Creator's promise of a peaceful and secure new world *before the generation that saw the events of 1914 passes away.*" After that date, the tract read: "Most important, this magazine builds confidence in the Creator's promise of a peaceful and secure world *that is about to replace the present wicked, lawless system of things.*" (emphasis mine)

The Art of Tacking

In 1981, as it ended an intense period of housecleaning during which, according to one account, 30,000 Witnesses left or were "disfellowshipped" (Mathew Schmalz in *Expecting Armageddon: Essential readings in failed prophecy*), the Watchtower Society spoke to the issue of seemingly erroneous prophecy:

"At times explanations have shown adjustments, seemingly to previous points of view. But this has not actually been the case."
—*Watchtower*, December 1981

In 1999, I knew nothing of the art of "tacking," although I knew more than I wanted to about "contrary winds." I only knew that I had spent my entire adult life preparing for the same thing at least two generations of Clarks had before me. The goal was ever the same…and yet, it continued to move further and further out of reach.

The Old Testament book of Deuteronomy is quite clear about the making of prophecy: "If what a prophet proclaims in the name of the Lord does not take place or come true, that is a message the Lord has not spoken. That prophet has spoken presumptuously. Do not be afraid of him." (Deuteronomy 18:22)

This verse has been applied to the Watchtower Society repeatedly throughout the years, and the organization has acknowledged that it doesn't always understand the complete and proper context of a prophecy until the events occur and an "increasing light" has shone on them.

"Does this admission of making mistakes stamp them [Watchtower] as false prophets?" asks *The Watchtower* (November 1972). It answers, "Not at all, for false prophets do not admit to making mistakes."

Ultimately, the Watchtower Society continues to associate itself with the Biblical verse about the "faithful and discreet

slave" that is dispensing spiritual food to mankind. Referring
to its own ministry, it states:

> "This 'faithful and discreet slave' was never inspired, never
> perfect. Let us never forget that the motives of this 'slave' were
> always pure, unselfish; at all times well-meaning."
>   —*Watchtower*, March 1979

The Faithful and Discreet Slave

Having read this far, you may be wondering on what authority
WTS doctrines rest and why, after so many disappointments,
the pattern of Kingdom Hall life continues. I can only tell you
what I was taught to believe. The authority, according to the
Watchtower Society, comes directly from the word of God,
which indicates that a true prophet—the Spirit of Truth—will
be sent to, as Jesus says, "guide you into all the truth" and
"declare to you the things coming." (John 16:12-15)

Who is this prophet?…This 'prophet' was not one man,
but was a body of men and women. It was the small group of
footstep followers of Jesus Christ…known as Jehovah's
Christian Witnesses… Of course, it is easy to say that this
group acts as a 'prophet' of God. It is another thing to prove it
                                    —*Watchtower*, April 1972

The Watchtower Society associates itself, then, not just with
the "faithful and discreet slave"—which it acknowledges is not
inspired—but with a being whose very purpose is to guide us
into all truth. Setting aside this paradox, it stands to reason
that an organization identifying itself as the "Spirit of Truth"
must be the "true church" of Christ.

This idea—that there is a True Church—has dominated Christian doctrine since the first efforts to organize the congregation. With the threat and promise of the second advent of Christ looming, it seems especially critical to be able to identify this True Church. It's no wonder the founders of the Watchtower Society were careful in determining the hallmarks of this divine organization.

Here they are, in short form:

- **The True Church must be unified.** Christ said there would be "one fold and one Shepherd," so the True Church couldn't be one of the many sects of Christianity already in existence, nor could it parrot their doctrines. This also meant there would be no priest class; the believers wouldn't be divided into leadership and laity (Matthew 20:25-28). Yes, Watchtower theology does include a "temple class" that dispenses the spiritual food to God's congregation, but this is not to be confused with a clergy.

- **The members of the True Church must have love among themselves** (I John 4:8). "For such love to be truly an identifying mark, it could not be merely a matter pretending to be nice to one another... It should influence how one treats the other members of one's household. It ought to affect one's attitude toward people of other races and nations." (*The Truth That Leads to Eternal Life*)

- **The members of the True Church must have respect for God's word.** This means taking the entire Bible as the inerrant word of God, adhering to the letter of its teachings, and exhorting others to do the same. The authoritative interpreters of this inerrant word are the aforementioned "faithful and discreet slave" class who head the Watchtower Society.

- **The True Church must proclaim the Kingdom of God** as man's true hope, because it is "his provision for governing the earth." In practice this means not just preaching the Kingdom to others, but decrying the efforts of other organizations that espouse humanitarian goals as promoting false hope and false religion.

- **The members of the True Church must separate themselves from the world and its affairs** (James 1:27). Anyone who is too friendly with "the world" is the enemy of God (James 4:4). Says the *Truth...* book: "You can appreciate why this is so serious when you remember that the Bible points out that the ruler of the world is God's chief adversary, Satan the Devil (John 15:19)." This means that the church and its members are not involved in politics, or in regional, national, or world affairs. They are not engaged in the human struggle here, because that struggle will soon be over.

- **The True Church must sanctify God's name.** Jesus says, "Our Father in the heavens, let your name be sanctified..." (Matthew 6:9) Obviously, then, it's important to know what that name is. Though Jesus Himself doesn't call His Divine Father "Jehovah" in this prayer, the Watchtower Society determined that Jehovah was the literal name of God and the only one to which He will answer. So the True Church must use this name. "Really, what group does bear witness to the name of God as Jesus did?" asks *Truth*. It answers, "There is only one people that notably follow Jesus' example in this regard."

These "requirements" of the True Church are laid out, reasoned through, and backed by scripture. A group that fails in just one of these requirements cannot claim to be the True Faith of God.

You might argue that any number of religious communities meet the criteria for unity, love, scriptural foundation, and holding God's name as sacred. Most forms of Christianity uphold the divine inspiration of the Bible; the Bahá'í Faith has no clergy and no sects, and teaches the unity of mankind; Buddhism urges detachment from the world; Hinduism looks to the coming of a Golden Age in the glory of a single, supreme God. But no matter how many criteria these faiths meet, they cannot—by definition—meet the last one. And that last criterion is a deal-breaker: there is only one faith that identifies itself exclusively with what its founders have determined is God's true and only name—Jehovah.

To someone on the inside, these criteria seem self-evident. They offer sanctuary, certainty, security, salvation, and structure in a world that sometimes appears to be coming apart at the seams. They extend the promise that whatever you may endure in life—disease, poverty, sorrow, loneliness—if you only are faithful to God's visible organization to the End and do its work, you'll be granted a place in the coming Paradise.

And if you don't, you'll be judged and found wanting.

These were the simple facts that pulled my prodigal feet to the straight path and kept them there throughout my adult life.

Table 1: A Timeline of Some WTS Prophecy

The table below shows the treatment of some of the dates targeted in Watchtower literature as "the End." Emphasis in the passages below is mine; the words of Christ are italicized.

Year	What Was Said	What Happened	WTS Response
1874	Charles Taze Russell accepted Adventist Jonas Wendell's calculation that 1874 would be the year of Christ's return.	Christ did not visibly appear on earth.	Russell taught that in 1874, Christ was invisibly present in the Heavenly Sanctuary: "Surely there is not the slightest room for doubt in the mind of a truly consecrated child of God that the Lord Jesus Christ is present and has been since 1874." *Watchtower,* January 1924
1914	"...we consider it **an established truth** that the final end of the kingdoms of this world, and **the full establishment of the Kingdom of God, will be accomplished** by the end of A.D. **1914**." — Charles Taze Russell	World War I began.	In 1914 Jesus began his rule in heaven. The evidence of this was the Great War itself. This turmoil was the beginning of the signs referred to by Jesus in Matthew 24:3-6: *"You are going to hear of wars and reports of wars; see that you are not terrified. For these things must take place, but the end is not yet."*
1915 - 1916	"In view of this strong Bible evidence concerning the Times of the Gentiles, we consider it **an established truth** that the final end of the kingdoms of this world, and **the full establishment of the kingdom of God, will be accomplished** near the end of A.D. **1915**." *The Time Is At Hand,* 1915	The Great War continued with governments still in power.	C.T. Russell died in 1916 and his writings were revamped to reflect the idea that the end of the Times of the Gentiles (at which time the Jews would be allowed to return to Jerusalem) merely *began* in 1914. In fact, the Jews were permitted to return to the Holy Land by official decree in 1844,
1918	"...in the year 1918, when God destroys the churches wholesale and the church members by millions, **it shall be** that any that escape shall come to the works of Pastor Russell to learn the meaning of the downfall of Christianity." *The Finished Mystery,* 1917	The Great War ended.	"The second coming of the Lord, therefore, **began** in 1874; and that date and the years 1914 and 1918 are specially marked dates with reference to his coming." *Creation,* 1927 Now the WTS introduced the idea that the End Times prophecies pointed to the generation "who saw the events of 1914." This refers to a prophecy in Matthew (24:34): *"Truly I say to you that **this generation will by no means pass away** until all these things occur."*

Year	What Was Said	What Happened	WTS Response
1925	"Therefore **we may confidently expect** that 1925 will mark the return of Abraham, Isaac, Jacob and the faithful prophets of old ... to the condition of human perfection." *Millions Now Living Will Never Die*	There did not seem to be a return of the "prophets of old" to "human perfection."	"It is to be expected that Satan will try to inject into the minds of the consecrated the thought that 1925 should see an end to the work." *Watchtower*, September 1925
	"Our thought is, that 1925 is **definitely settled** by the Scriptures." *Watchtower*, April 1923	There was a falling away of believers at this time.	"Some anticipated that the work would end in 1925, but the Lord did not state so. The difficulty was that **the friends inflated their imaginations beyond reason;** and that when their imaginations burst asunder, they were inclined to throw away everything." *Watchtower* 1926
1931	"God's ... day of vengeance is here and Armageddon is at hand and certain to fall upon Christendom and that **within an early date**. God's judgment is upon Christendom and **must shortly be executed**." J. F. Rutherford, *Vindication*, Vol. I, 1931	"...the faithful ... learned to stop fixing dates for the future and predicting what would come to pass on a certain date..." *Vindication*, 1931	Despite words about "fixing dates," this still led to an expectation that Christendom would be overthrown in 1932.
1935	"...the scriptural evidence and the physical facts **strongly indicate** that such witness work is now almost done; and when it is done the universal war will begin. ...**during the few remaining months** until the breaking of that universal cataclysm the powers that rule the nations of the earth will continue to make treaties..." *Universal War Near*, 1935	Months passed without universal war being realized.	Though no firm date was set, there was till a general sense of an impending event.
1938 - 1945	"[T]he words of Jesus ... **definitely seem to discourage the bearing of children** immediately before or during Armageddon. ...there is no reasonable or scriptural injunction to bring children into the world immediately before Armageddon, **where we now are**." *Watchtower*, November 1938 The book *Children* by J.F. Rutherford is referred to as "... the Lord's provided instrument for most effective work **in the remaining months before Armageddon**." *Watchtower* September, 1941	The US became a combatant in World War II in 1941, but heavenly forces were not engaged.	Attention turns to the United Nations, which is seen "as one of the most positive evidences that 'the kingdom of heaven is at hand' and that the end of the world arrangement is now near. Jesus foretold the setting up of **that anti-Christ organization**." *The Kingdom Is at Hand*, 1944

Year	What Was Said	What Happened	WTS Response
1946 - 1961	General prophecies about how close the End is continued to be made, but no specific dates were given.	The world stumbled onward...	Warnings were given about "those in times past who predicted an end to the world, even announcing a specific date. Yet nothing happened." What was missing from these prophecies? asks *Awake!* magazine in October 1968. It answers that these people lacked: "...God's truths and evidence that he was using and guiding them."
1975	"According to this trustworthy Bible chronology six thousand years from man's creation will end in 1975... The reign of Christ" will "run parallel with the 7th millennium ..." *Life Everlasting in Freedom of the Sons of God*, 1966	1975 passed without the battle of Armageddon concluding.	The WTS acknowledged that "...some who have been serving God have planned their lives according to **a mistaken view of just what was to happen on a certain date or in a certain year**. They may have, for this reason, **put off or neglected things that they otherwise would have cared for**. But they have missed the point of the Bible's warnings concerning the end of this system of things, thinking that Bible chronology reveals the specific date." *Watchtower*, July 1976 This was followed by several years of turmoil during which 30,000 Witnesses were "dis-fellowshipped."
1994 - 2004	"...Jesus said: '*This generation will by no means pass away until all these things occur* [including the end of this system].' Which generation did Jesus mean? **He meant the generation of people who were living in 1914.** Those persons yet remaining of that generation are now very old. However, some of them will still be alive to see the end of this wicked system. So **of this we can be certain**: Shortly now there will be a sudden end to all wickedness and wicked people at Armageddon." *You Can Live Forever In Paradise On Earth*, 1982	The generation alive in 1914 came and went and still Armageddon had not occurred. The world was still there. I left the Kingdom Hall in 1999.	Discussing the generation of Matthew 24, the November 1995 *Watchtower* says Jesus' prophecy about "*this generation*": "apparently refers to the peoples of earth (now) who see the signs of Christ's presence but fail to mend their ways."

IV

Heaven and Hell

Unwholesome Associations

By the time I reached high school, our family's history of
inconstancy in the Kingdom Hall was pretty well established.
Given Dad's work schedule, we attended very few meetings
and didn't participate at all in Field Service. We boys ran a little wild—especially Keith.

As if to make up for this spiritual laxity, our parents chose
teachings of the Kingdom Hall seemingly at random to be
adamant about. We did not celebrate birthdays or Christmas,
and we were not allowed the sort of extra-curricular activities
that most kids take for granted. I discovered this the hard way
in high school, when I inadvertently tested the boundaries of
my parents' dedication to Watchtower doctrine.

I tried out for and was accepted into my high school
wrestling and cross-country teams. I can't begin to describe

what this meant to me: To earn a "letter" for a sport, to win awards for my abilities, to *be* somebody among my peers...to make my father proud of me. It was with this thrilling prospect filling my head and heart that I arrived home one afternoon with a duffel bag full of my school-issued sports gear and a list of things my parents needed to buy.

Dad, far from being proud that his son had managed to make not one but *two* sports teams, was furious. "Take it back!" he told me. "Take the equipment back! You're not going to do sports!"

"But why?" I asked. "It's not expensive."

"It's dangerous," Dad told me. But the risks he envisioned were not just to life and limb, they were to my soul and my chances of eternal life.

To participate in sports I would have to associate with kids who were not Jehovah's Witnesses—"worldly youths," in other words. Association with these "outsiders," Dad reminded me, should be limited to trying to convert them. Otherwise my association with them was "unwholesome."

He backed this with Watchtower doctrine: "Any recreation you take outside of school should not be with worldly youths." (*Watchtower* September 1964)

"I don't want you to have unwholesome associations," Dad told me.

"Could I do *one* sport?" I asked, and picked my favorite. "Wrestling?"

"Wrestling is a violent sport! Do you have any idea what would happen if you did a violent sport? You could be injured, for one thing. And you could be disfellowshipped."

Disfellowshipped. The ultimate humiliation.

I took the equipment back to the team coaches and

withdrew, telling them simply that my family couldn't afford to have me take the time after school.

Even without sports I managed to fall into "unwholesome associations." Literally.

I wasn't a ninety-eight pound weakling as a teen, but I was smaller than average and tended to be very shy. This combination was pretty much like wearing a sign on my back that read: *Kick me.* I collected more than my share of "noogies," "wedgies," and other indignities throughout high school…up until I met Wade in my senior year.

I was in the hallway during a class change when a bigger, tougher, meaner kid named Greg decided I needed to be put in my place—that is, face down on the floor. He had grabbed me by the collar, shoved me up against the lockers, and pulled his arm back for the knock-out punch when a big, muscular hand appeared on his shoulder and an impossibly deep voice said, "What's your problem, dip-shit?"

My tormentor looked up over his shoulder into a face that seemed to be carved of pitted sandstone. He glowered. "*He's* my problem," he said, nodding toward me. "He's a wimp."

"*He's* a wimp? He's not the one getting ready to pound a guy half his size." The newcomer shook Greg like a dog worrying a bone. "Why don't you let go…wimp?"

I think Greg—who was into body-building, I should note—meant to utter some scathing comeback. I'm sure he wanted to anyway, but the big guy literally wrenched him to his knees on the highly polished floor.

"Beg me not to kill you," he said, completely deadpan.

"C'mon, Wade…" Greg protested. "Lemme up."

"Beg!" Wade commanded.

A detached part of my mind was fascinated by this exchange.

Though not as tall, Greg was easily as buff as Wade and might have been able to hold his own in a fight, but he was terrified. I could smell his terror, see it oozing out of his sallow skin.

He begged. "Please don't kill me, Wade," he mumbled.

Wade smiled. "You're gonna be late to class," he said and gave Greg a playful shove that sent him sprawling.

David scrambled away and the crowd dispersed.

Wade turned to me, still smiling, and said, "Hi, I'm Wade. That guy's a pussy, isn't he?"

I agreed quickly, "Yes, he is."

It was a true case of opposites attracting. Wade was everything I was not. He was massive—tall and big-boned—and muscled like a prize bull. He was also secure in his own person, comfortable in his skin, and certain of his opinion about everything. And for whatever reason, he took me—shy and insecure and uncertain as I was—under his brawny wing.

We became friends—no, more than friends—partners in crime. We were an enforcement team, roaming the halls intimidating the hell out of our fellow students. (Well, Wade did most of the intimidating, but he sometimes let me pick the target.) We made nice, chrome *nunchuks* with which to do our intimidating and practiced our moves anywhere there was an audience.

An oversized native American and an undersized white boy, we were still odd-ducks of a feather—a couple of hopeless misfits who found some sort of validation in each other's company. To me, Wade was a being from another planet. I don't know what I was to him. But I apparently had something he needed and he certainly fulfilled some need in me.

Wade was responsible for a number of firsts in my life—some instructive, some destructive. Perhaps the most profound was set in motion the day he asked me if I'd ever had a drink. It took me a moment to realize he was talking about alcohol, and at seventeen, I was embarrassed to admit that I hadn't.

"I'd like to someday, though," I said. "Just to see how it feels."

"It feels great," he assured me. "Come over to my house Friday after school and I'll show you. My parents are gonna be gone for the evening."

Friday couldn't come soon enough. During the week I peppered Wade with questions about what it felt like to have a "beer buzz."

"It just relaxes you," he said, which, looking back, I realize was a big deal to someone as tightly wound as Wade.

Though I could have asked for a ride from my big brother Don, when Friday finally rolled around I opted to walk the two miles to Wade's house. It had snowed about two feet the day before and the afternoon was beautiful, bright, glistening, and peaceful. But inside, I was exploding with anticipation of my first beer. I think I ran the last hundred yards to Wade's front door. I knocked, and there he was, his acne-scored face wearing a big grin.

"Are you ready for a drink?" he asked.

"Yes, I am," I said and followed him into the house.

In the kitchen, he swung wide the refrigerator door…and I thought I was going to die. On the shelf was not the one little can of beer I had expected to perhaps share, but two quart-sized bottles—one for each of us. I don't believe I spoke for the next minute or two, but my brain bleated, *You can't drink that!*

Wade got us each a glass and handed me my bottle and we started to drink.

The smell hit me first. It was *horrible*. Like essence of swamp. I touched the beer to my lips. It tasted even worse. Like…I didn't want to put a name to what it tasted like.

Wade was watching me, a veiled smile in his dark eyes. "Just gulp it and try not to taste it," he told me. "Bottoms up!" He demonstrated.

I held my breath, tilted the glass up and chugged, not stopping until it was empty.

Wade was proud of me. I could see it in his eyes. He refilled his glass. I refilled mine. We toasted each other, then forced ourselves to swallow glass after glass until the two quarts of beer was gone.

As we guzzled, Wade told jokes so funny I couldn't stop laughing. We laughed until our sides hurt. That was when the afternoon took a bizarre turn.

We started horsing around, wrestling. This was something I knew pretty well, even though I'd never gotten to join the school wrestling team. Full of beer, I felt competent, powerful, in command. I wanted to show Wade that I wasn't just a shy, gawky white boy. I was strong and coordinated. I'd show him. I'd prove myself.

I found I could pin him easily—far more easily than I expected. It didn't occur to me to chalk it up to the fact that he was also full of beer, or that the beer buzz made him mellow. I took it as proof positive that I was quicker, stronger than my big, tough Native American buddy.

He's a fake, I thought as I locked him in wrestling holds again and again. *He's weak. He's a burn-out—big, but clumsy as hell. Are all Indians like this,* I let myself wonder, *strong but unable to fight?*

I don't know if he somehow caught what I was thinking or

saw it in my face, or if he suddenly realized I wasn't kidding around anymore. Whatever the reason, he let out a howl—an adrenaline-filled, wild Indian war-whoop. His eyes rolled back in his head. Then suddenly he was on his feet, towering over me. He grabbed his chrome *nunchuks* so fast his arm looked like a bolt of copper lightening. Before I could react, he swung the weapon in a vicious arc that ended on top of my head. In an instant I was face down on the floor.

He kicked me twice in the ribs and said, "I'll fucking kill you if you try that again!"

A glance at his face convinced me that he meant it, and for a moment I thought he *would* kill me. Terrified, I began to cry, holding my head. My hair was wet and warm. I pulled my hands away from my head and stared at them. I was bleeding.

In the moment of complete stillness that followed, I heard Wade's *nunchuks* hit the floor.

"Shit, Bro," he said. "We're just fuckin' around, right Dan? Right, Bro?"

I dared to look up at him again. His face was ashen beneath its coppery blush.

"Yeah," I said. "Just fuckin' around. We're forever. You're my Bro, right?"

He smiled. "Right. Sorry, man."

I forgave him instantly, and he showered me with brotherly affection.

I have a difficult time understanding that incident to this day. In the span of five minutes, I went from feeling as if my best friend hated me enough to kill me to basking in the warmth of his love. He *cared* for me. I was his brother. He'd said it. I could forgive almost anything for that.

The whole episode had taken an hour, maybe two. It was

not quite dark by the time I decided I should leave. When I opened the front door of Wade's house, it was as if I had opened the door to heaven. The snow glistened with the white of diamonds, as if a sheer, jeweled veil had been laid over everything.

I leapt from the front porch and began running through the snow, scattering the jewels. In the grip of a strange, wonderful euphoria, I didn't feel the cold. I jumped through drifts and fell and rolled in the glorious treasure, and could not feel a thing. I was at peace, blissful, satisfied. I had never felt so wonderful.

I finally ran down and then sat down. The laughter bubbling up from inside me stilled. I felt as if I were on a Merry-Go-Round—my head spun. I closed my eyes, but it wouldn't stop—the world merely spun faster and faster. I couldn't stand up.

At that point what bubbled up from inside wasn't laughter. I rolled over in the snow and retched up all the beer I'd drunk. Then, spent and empty, I began the long walk home in the suddenly freezing twilight.

For some teenagers the signal event of high school is the first date, the senior prom, the sports trophy, the first driver's license, or some academic award. That afternoon with Wade was my signal event. My defining moment. I didn't know it at the time, but I had just become addicted to alcohol.

Genevieve

After I graduated from high school, Dad no longer insisted I go to meetings at the Kingdom Hall. "You're an adult," he told me. "All I ask of you if you're going to live in this house is that you don't come home drunk."

I wasn't sure I could keep that promise, so I looked for ways to get out on my own—Ior at least to get out of my parents' house.

Though we were inconstant Witnesses, doctrine ran deep; there had been no thought given to my higher education. Our theology disallowed it. *Watchtower* magazine had warned my parents that though my school might have student counselors who "encourage one to pursue a higher education" or "a career with a future in the current system of things," we were not to be persuaded by their arguments.

Said the Watchtower:

"Do not be influenced by them. Do not let them brainwash you with the Devil's propaganda to get ahead" (*Watchtower,* March 1969)

Instead of seeking a career, the young Witness was expected to pursue missionary work. "In view of the short time left," advised *The Kingdom Ministry* (June 1969), " a decision to pursue a career in this system of things is not only unwise but extremely dangerous... Many young Brothers and Sisters were offered scholarships, or employment that promised fine pay. However, they turned them down and put spiritual interests first."

But at nineteen, I was unbaptized and not at all inclined to "spiritual interests." I was also unskilled, untrained, and had no glimmer of a calling or profession. I learned to hang drywall and left home with a high school buddy, bound for Houston, Texas. We moved in with my brother Keith and his wife Marie, and there we stayed for about six months while we hung drywall every day and drank every night.

One of Keith's friends, Tim, had also moved to Texas from Michigan and, as fate or Divine Providence would have it, was also a drywall guy. He also drank quite a bit, which gave us a number of things in common and led to a friendship of sorts.

One day at work Tom informed me that his girlfriend had flown down from Michigan to visit him and was staying at his house. He invited me over to meet her, of course, and I was beyond surprise to realize that I already knew her. Her name was Genevieve, her parents were from France, and I had been smitten with her in high school, though I'd never had the guts to ask her out. Now here she was—my friend's girlfriend.

But Tom confided in me that he was in rather a dilemma. Since coming to Houston, he'd met another girl who he liked better than Genevieve, and wasn't quite sure what to do about it. What he did was abandon poor Gen pretty much altogether. That not only bewildered her and hurt her feelings, but it put me in a dilemma of my own. As far as Gen was concerned she was still Tom's girl and hardly free to be courted by one of his buddies. To me she was fair game.

So I wooed her without seeming to woo. We hung out together, with or without Tom, and I made my best effort to be witty, funny, endearing, and available.

One evening, while the three of us were out drinking at *Mickey Gilley's* in Pasadena, Texas, Tom took me aside in the bar and said, "Look, man, she's all yours—you can have her."

"Okay," I said eloquently.

Somehow the message also got to Genevieve that night that she was being cut loose. But she wasn't hurt; she was perfectly happy. She hopped into my lap on the way home and seemed content to stay there. We fell in love on the spot. I don't recall what happened to Tom and his new girlfriend, but Gen and I were an item.

About a month after we renewed our acquaintance, Gen talked me into moving back to Michigan with her. She had a job there, and was sure I could find construction work, so I went north and moved in with Genevieve.

She was Catholic, as it happened—a lapsed Catholic in much the same way that I was a lapsed Jehovah's Witness. She'd been raised in the faith, but had fallen away. We started talking a little bit about religion, and, to my surprise, she expressed some interest in understanding what the Watchtower Society was about.

I knew an Elder in the area named Brian and contacted him on her behalf. He suggested that she read one of the Watchtower publications. As a result, Gen decided to study with Brian at our apartment. Despite my fitful relationship with the Kingdom Hall, I was pleased by this turn of events. I decided I'd sit in on the study sessions myself, maybe bone up on all the stuff I'd paid so little attention to as a kid.

But when I announced my intention, Brian stated flatly that I couldn't study with them because I was committing adultery with Gen. He could study with *her*, he explained to us, because she was uninformed—she didn't know the Biblical teachings on immorality from the WTS perspective. I, on the other hand, knew better. I had become one of those "unwholesome associations" that Jehovah's Witnesses are to avoid.

If I wanted to study the faith, Brian suggested, Genevieve and I should stop living in sin and get married.

We did.

I suppose I had visions of us getting baptized together—becoming a couple in the Kingdom Hall and a door-to-door team. God and circumstance dictated otherwise.

V

A JW Through-and-Through

The Loneliest Number

We moved back to Houston after the wedding. I couldn't find work in Michigan's soft housing market and I had no other skills. In Houston, there was at least work for me. I could support my new wife.

Genevieve's mother visited us not long after the move. She was very French, and *very* Catholic. To her daughter she said (and I'm paraphrasing), "You're a married woman now. You may be having kids soon. Get your butt signed up at the local Catholic church so they get raised in the faith."

Gen, who was terrified of her mama (and rightfully so) convinced me that we should enroll in adult catechism classes. This seemed fair to me. She'd studied the faith of my fathers; I should reciprocate.

It didn't work, of course. The doctrines of the Catholic

Church seemed confusing and contradictory to me, but even worse in my eyes was the fact that Gen started smoking after class with our Catechism instructor. It wasn't long before she was smoking all the time.

I didn't want to be Catholic, I decided. And Gen clearly didn't want to be a Jehovah's Witness. She would remain a Catholic; I determined that I would be nothing. For Gen's sake I tried to celebrate Christmas and birthdays and other holidays, but I had been taught from birth that these things were not acceptable to Jehovah. The belief was so ingrained that when I did these things with my wife, though I tried my best, my heart was not in it. In fact, I felt just plain *wrong*. And she knew it.

"You're a JW through-and-through," she told me one night in the heat of an argument.

I didn't want to hear that. "Give me another chance," I begged her. I made promises I knew I couldn't keep—I'd throw myself into important celebrations, I'd try studying the Catholic faith again, I'd go to mass.

But my protests didn't convince Gen any more than they convinced me. I discovered she'd already found someone else and, after one-and-a-half years of marriage, our relationship crumbled.

In the aftermath, feeling like an utter failure, I realized Gen was right: I was a JW through-and-through.

I Take Hold of the Truth

The ink hadn't dried on the divorce decree when my brother Keith went into action, requesting that the Elders of his Kingdom Hall pay me a visit. They brought consolation and support; they offered clarity and hope. Of course my marriage had failed, they told me: I had strayed from God's visible organization. I had married an outsider, an unbeliever. I had been living in sin. I had let myself be seduced by the world. There could have been no other conceivable outcome.

Boiled down to its essentials, the message was clear: I had done this to myself.

But there was a remedy: I could be baptized, return to the Kingdom Hall, and be assured that I would soon have my life back together. I should forget about Genevieve, let go of my futile love for her. In the Kingdom Hall were any number of fine, godly "Sisters" who would be eager to marry me as soon as I had taken hold of the truth once and for all.

They weren't kidding. I'd no sooner expressed an interest in returning to the Kingdom Hall when the Sisters literally stood in line, vying for dates, bringing food and gifts to my apartment, visiting me alone there though it was against the rules; I was not a baptized Brother, they weren't supposed to associate with me. But they did. Some even drank with me. And I took full advantage, dating three or four of them at a time, letting them compete for a place in my life.

I was angry, then—angry for a number of reasons I barely understood. I was angry at Gen for betraying and leaving me, for ruining my life. Possibly I was even angry at her for falling in love with me and at myself for falling for her. I was definitely angry at myself for failing at marriage. My parents had a terribly difficult relationship, but *they'd* never divorced, never given up on each other. How could I be so inept as to fail after little more than a year, having sustained so few real tests? I was angry at the Elders who were trying to bring me back into the fold—surely they saw me as a loser. And those Sisters who courted me so persistently—couldn't they see the big, fat "L" on my forehead?

I was ashamed. Ashamed to have fallen out of my faith. Ashamed to have been "seduced" by the world. Ashamed to be the first in my family to be divorced.

And so I marshaled all my courage and went back to the Kingdom Hall for my first meeting in five years. I came back to Jehovah full strength, studying all the publications, internalizing the doctrine, and finally, getting baptized. Within one year, I was elevated to the position of ministerial servant, charged with handling the microphones for meetings, reading *The Watchtower* before the congregation, and handing out magazines in the Bookroom. I even went on "shepherding calls" with the Elders. And, of course, I had my pick of single women for my next marriage.

I was a lucky, God-kissed guy who once again heard the countdown to The End.

VI

Prodigal at the Door

Reasoning from the Scripture

The year or so after the dissolving of my marriage was a mixed bag. As if to balance the quivering sense of loss I experienced with Genevieve gone, I felt as if I were part of a big family, socializing with Elders and fellow brethren, training with them for Field Service calls, learning the ropes of being a Jehovah's Witness again.

Training for Field Service was my least favorite aspect of my return, I suppose. I was not a naturally outgoing person and I went into the training feeling that I was out of my element. But led by practiced Elders, we studied the New World Translation of the Bible together with Watchtower Bible tracts and books, learning how to "reason from the scriptures" with those we visited. Special attention was given to handling those who were too knowledgeable about the scriptures—or at least more knowledgeable than we were—and overcoming "conversation stoppers" such as "I have my own religion, thanks" or "I don't believe in organized religion." We often did role-playing exercises to practice for the real world work, drilling each other on how to conduct a home visit.

After a few months of this sort of weekly study, I made my first foray into Field Service at the ripe old age of twenty-four. Though paired with an experienced Brother who I knew would do the "heavy lifting" during our calls, I was still tremendously nervous. I had heard all the horror stories: people setting their dogs on Witnesses, slamming the door in their faces, becoming verbally abusive, flaunting evidences of an occult or immoral lifestyle, showing evidences of deep scholarship. The best I could hope for, it seemed, was polite disinterest, so I hoped for that.

As I said, I—like any "newbie"—was paired with an experienced Brother. My role was to hand out literature, pray for the success of the visit, and read from scripture when so instructed by my partner. I don't remember much about that first day of Field Service work, which is testimony to its uneventfulness, I guess. What I *do* remember is that my partner praised me to the rafters afterward in the post-service meeting at which we compared notes with other teams. He spoke of how I had overcome my fears, smilingly handed out literature, and read appropriate scripture.

It was a proud moment, and I had known few enough of those in my life. I was now a "publisher" within the congregation. (This is a reference to Isaiah 52:7: "How comely upon the mountains are the feet of the one bringing good news, the one *publishing peace*, the one bringing good news of something better, the one publishing salvation, the one saying to Zion: 'Your God has become king!'")

Knock and It Shall Be Opened

This positive reinforcement notwithstanding, my feelings about Field Service were conflicted. Ninety percent of the time I was nervous, fearful, my guard up—ready for the door to slam, the dog to bite, the unexpected to happen. Jehovah's Witnesses were seldom welcome. We were perpetually bothering people, catching them in the middle of things. We interrupted their spiritual pursuits—prayer meetings or meditations—we pulled them away from family gatherings, work, meals, sleep, phone calls.

Even when we were invited into the front hall, they were distracted by what was going on in the home—the needs of children, a news broadcast or TV show, music on the stereo, worry over what the family cat was up to or what had become of that pot of soup they left on the stove.

And there might be dangers within the home itself to contend with. Was the music we heard playing in the background demonic rock & roll? Was that statuette in the hallway an iconic image of some pagan god? Was there a crucifix with a dead Christ staring us in the face? Would we be subjected to heathen scripture? What about that painting—might it be venting demonic energy into the home? Indeed, were there demonic elements present that we couldn't see?

Demons are very much alive in Watchtower theology and are believed to exert a real influence in the world, entering unwary people's lives through music, art, and cultural artifacts. One of my most memorable brushes with the demonic was with a Brother named Darryl who had come to the Kingdom Hall at the end of a strange and violent path that included (if Darryl's own accounts can be believed) occult worship and the deaths of many small animals. One afternoon while out with Darryl I was pleased to actually be invited into the home of a pleasant fellow who seemed open to discussion with us. We'd no sooner stepped through the door than Darryl stiffened.

"There are demons here," he said in a voice that made my hair stand on end.

The homeowner gaped at him in offended silence, and before I could mumble an apology and excuse us, Darryl grasped my arm, turned me around, and hustled me out of the house.

I was torn between mortification and terror. "What do you mean, there are demons here?" I stammered.

"What I said," Darryl said stonily. "There are demons in that house."

"How do you know?"

"I have experience with demons," Darryl told me, straight-faced. "In fact, I once had a belt that was demon-possessed. When I wore it I could lift a *huge* amount of weight—weight that should have crushed me. Trust me—I can smell demons."

I did not return to the "demon-infested" house with Darryl or any other partner. I put the homeowner on a "don't call" list.

While this was probably the strangest of my experiences in Field Service, it was not the most outright terrifying. That honor goes to a call in which a pioneer Sister and I were invited into the home of a man who dead-bolted the door behind us the moment we crossed his threshold. It was only when I turned to look at the door that I realized there was a rifle propped behind it.

Unease lumping in my throat, I led with the opening sally of the day—I don't remember what it was—and he answered with a tirade about patriotism. He had recently been to a baseball game, he told us, at which a scattering of un-American sons-of-bitches had refused to rise and sing the national anthem. He told us what he thought should happen to those traitorous souls, then asked what we thought about such behavior.

I am sure he knew that Jehovah's Witnesses neither sing the national anthem nor recite the Pledge of Allegiance, and that we consider the flag to be a manmade idol or graven image. My companion and I desperately hid our terror and, quivering between this glowering fellow and his rifle, we calmly shared our views on patriotism and the flag, then politely excused ourselves to rejoin our waiting brethren in the car that sat at the end of his driveway.

He gave us one last smoldering look, then opened the door and allowed us to escape. It may have been my imagination that I heard laughter as we made our way down his driveway.

I had really started to get into the swing of things when I encountered what was probably the most significant of my early Field Service experiences—one in which I was thrown head first into one of our role-playing scenarios. It was significant because it completely up-ended my hard-won confidence.

On this Saturday morning my female partner and I were greeted at the door of one home by a sweet-faced older woman who smilingly invited us in. She ushered us to seats in her living room where her husband held court from an over-stuffed chair.

She had no sooner introduced us to him, than he said, "Bring the Word."

She immediately excused herself and returned moments later with the biggest Bible I have ever seen. She announced, "My husband will now teach you from the book of Daniel."

While we stared at each other in confusion, the woman handed the huge tome to her husband, who caused it to open to the book of Daniel as if it had been trained at Bible Obedience School. He cleared his throat and began to preach to us about the prophecies in the Old Testament book.

I was flummoxed, completely and utterly undone. I had no idea what to say. Everything I'd learned in our role-playing exercises flew right out of my head, and I knew without a doubt that this man had forgotten more about the Bible than I had ever known. I was out of my depth.

Fortunately, my fellow publisher was more experienced than I at this sort of thing. When the old fellow at last paused to take a breath, she stepped neatly in and used something he had said as a stepping-off point for her own comments on Daniel. She set forth the Watchtower teachings on the subject of prophecy, stressing our love for Christ and our belief in the promises of His return. Then she politely excused us—we had people waiting for us, after all.

I came back from this episode utterly humiliated. My confidence evaporated with the realization that, for all my study, I knew next to nothing about the Bible. My knowledge was all rote. I didn't dare stray outside the lines I had learned, because to do so revealed that I was hopelessly ignorant about the very Book I claimed was the basis of my faith.

"I'm a fake," I told a Brother I saw as both successful and knowledgeable. "I don't know the Bible! What can I possibly hope to accomplish out there if there are people like that who know so much more than I do? I'm never going door-to-door again."

"Dan, it doesn't matter what you know or don't know. I don't know that much more than you do. But I *do* know the secret of Field Service. And that is that you don't have to engage anyone you don't want to. All you have to do is share *The Watchtower* and *Awake!*. You don't have to talk about what they want to talk about. If they want to discuss something you're not prepared to speak to, you just give them a big smile and offer to come back next week to talk about *that*. And in between, you study up on the subject. When you come back the next time, you're an expert. Then if they spring something else on you at *that* meeting you do the same thing: just say, 'That's an interesting subject. I'll be happy to discuss it with you next time.'"

I took his advice to heart and continued my work in Field Service as we were all commanded to do.

Never Enough

On balance, there were also positive teaching experiences—visits during which people invited us into their homes with warmth and kindness, expressed real interest, accepted our magazines and asked for books, accepted our books and asked for Bible studies. But somehow even the most profoundly successful experiences carried an undertone of negativity.

I once had a series of visits with a lovely, but poor black family in Nacogdoches who invited me to hold weekly Bible studies in their home. They had next to nothing, so the Biblical promises and *Watchtower* artists' renderings of the future I laid out before them looked *very* good indeed. It occurred to me for the first time, I think, that these were really the only people who saw the teachings on world destruction and rebirth as a promise rather than a threat. They had nothing to lose in this

life. Anything was better than their daily struggle to keep food
on the table, to clothe and educate their children and preserve
them from drugs and violence.

I felt good about bringing the Gospel to these people,
make no mistake, but far from feeling a sense of "rightness"
before my God, my overwhelming emotion was despair. No
matter how much I did, I could never do enough. God,
according to the *Watchtower* theology, only accepts our very
best and we, being sinful, broken beings, are incapable of giving Him that. So, for every hour I put into the activities of the
Kingdom Hall, I knew I should be putting in two. And even
when I *did* put in more, it still felt like too little.

I found myself in a vicious and depressing cycle of frantic
activity, blame, and sickening dread. And I was not alone. I
looked around me and realized that my friends and family
within the Kingdom Hall were all, to one degree or another,
caught up in the same cycle. I had only to look at my brothers
or my father. These men felt their lack of spiritual capacity so
keenly that they sidelined work, family, and health to put more
effort toward trying to rescue souls from the looming destruction of the world and bring them into life everlasting.

Naturally, at some point, this neglect of those "worldly"
concerns would pay negative dividends—their marriages
rocked, their children felt neglected, their houses, work, and
health fell into disrepair—and they would be cautioned by the
Elders of their congregation to take care of what needed taking
care of. This, of course, meant they had to cut back on such
things as Field Service or attendance at the weekly meetings,
which would also bring about shepherding by the Elders.

You couldn't, as the saying goes, win for losing. And as
smug as some people can be about being "saved," the scriptures

offered no guarantees. Even after the hours of door-to-door teaching, the years of meetings and Book Studies, and striving to do Jehovah's will, the earnest believer is left with only a *probability* of attaining Paradise. For Zephaniah says, "Seek righteousness, seek meekness. *Probably* you may be concealed in the day of Jehovah's anger."

Still, we soldiered on—*I* soldiered on—repeating the same acts that never brought spiritual peace, somehow expecting that they some day miraculously *would* bring peace. Sometime later, I realized that that is one definition of insanity: repeating the same futile actions over and over, but expecting different results. In view of my mother's illness the realization was unsettling.

At the time, I contented myself with what I could legitimately claim to have accomplished. I did a lot of door-to-door witnessing. I brought people to the faith or at least got them to listen to its principles. I might never earn Jehovah's approval, I reasoned, but my efforts in teaching His faith brought me bragging rights in His organization. I might not ever win Jehovah's love, but I had at least won the respect of my fellow Witnesses.

VII

A Marriageable Man

Sisters

Along with the respect of my peers, I also had won the full attention of every marriageable woman in my Kingdom Hall. The several that lived in my apartment complex must have thought they had an advantage over the others, but that wasn't the case. If anything, they were too much, too soon—I felt like Gold Rush California, overrun with zealous miners all desperate (*too* desperate) to stake a claim.

I wasn't even half-serious about pairing up again until I found myself in a Book Study group with two attractive Sisters, Renée and Andrea. I gave them very little more than shy glances when we first were introduced, but the wife of the Elder who led the group contrived at every turn to call my attention to them or engage us together in dialogue.

As I said, they were attractive young women. Both were

beautiful with fair hair, blue eyes, and winning smiles. Renée struck me as being a bit worldly and wild—like an untamed horse straining at the lead. Andrea, by contrast, was more serene and more down-to-earth. It was Andrea I found most appealing. She seemed more stable than Renée, more of a hearth-and-home kind of girl—a good helpmate.

Still, I wasn't ready for courtship. My history with Genevieve had left me cautious, suspicious of my own feelings, and reluctant to bind myself to another woman. I had no intention of opening myself up again to the sort of raw agony losing Gen had put me through. I meant to take the advice of my peers to choose wisely among the field of available options. When I married again, it would be a matter of practicality, I told myself, not an affair of the heart. So, I saw no reason to jump into a relationship with either of the two young women who stood at the top of my "A-list."

This was a source of great disappointment among my fellow Jehovah's Witnesses who wanted to see me safely paired off. By safely, of course, I mean yoked with someone within the organization. When my brother Don's five-year-old daughter died from complications from cerebral palsy (an event that drew him back into the Kingdom Hall after long absence), and I returned to Michigan to attend her funeral, I discovered that this fear for my spiritual safety extended to my immediate family as well.

At the funeral, I received a surprise in the form of an old high school girlfriend who came up to me after the service to renew acquaintances. The attraction between us was immediate and electric. This did not escape the notice of my Uncle Nick. As I passed down the receiving line at the reception, he grasped my hand in his and would not let go.

All but crushing it, he growled, "Throw her to the dogs!"

I don't know what my face was doing as I stared up at him, but my mind was racing, scrambling for meaning. It took me a startled instant to recognize the reference to the Biblical story of Jezebel, one of history's most treacherous and notoriously immoral women. I realized at once that the "her" to whom he referred was my old girlfriend, Brenda.

As I struggled to pull my bruised hand away, he continued, "I can crush your hand, Dan, but Jehovah can crush your soul."

He let go of me and I fled. But I made my excuses to Brenda and spent my time in the safe bosom of my family.

I was a bit surprised—not to say worried—when Uncle Nick invited me to drive back to Georgia with him and his family for a visit. I'm not sure why I accepted. It seemed the right thing to do at the time. We drove straight through the night while Nick and his family read from the Bible and Watchtower tracts and spoke to me endlessly about Jehovah and the work of His visible organization.

Preaching to the choir? Yes, and it occurred to me to wonder at first why they were doing it. Had my attraction to Brenda gotten Nick that worried about the strength of my faith? Was this something in the nature of an intervention? Then I realized that all the time they spent talking to me during the drive counted toward the hours they were expected to put in "pioneering" each month. I relaxed a bit and let the conversation slide over and around me. I joined in now and again and stopped culling through their words for veiled warnings. Still I was relieved when at last we arrived at their home in Georgia…that is, until my uncle introduced me—with a wink and a nod—to the young, but already toothless female mechanic who worked on his cars.

"Ruth," he was quick to tell me, "is a Sister in our local Kingdom Hall. She may not be a beauty, but she's a hard-working girl. A man could do worse. You should get to know her while you're here."

"I can't," I told him. "I already have someone—back in Houston."

"Yeah? What's her name?"

"Actually," I said, "there are these two sisters—Renée and Andrea. I like both of them."

Uncle Nick speared me with a glance and growled, "They all have the same working parts, boy. Pick one and make it work."

Pick One and Make it Work

Just like that. *Pick one and make it work.* It may seem outrageous advice to the "outsider," and awfully demeaning to the women in my life, but among the Jehovah's Witnesses of my acquaintance, marriage was less about personal happiness than it was about contributing to the resources of the Kingdom Hall. It was also considered a temporary situation at best. The world would soon end and we would be changed.

Besides, I had to own that I hadn't done so well marrying for *love*.

I decided that I'd waited long enough. It was time for me to go home and tie the knot with *somebody*, thus ending the world's impatient wait for Dan Clark to come to his senses. I told God I'd let Him decide who that somebody would be. I'd go back to Houston and marry whichever of the two girls picked me up at the bus station.

It wasn't until I was preparing to make the call for a ride

that I realized it was Andrea I liked best. I gave up on my coin toss and called her apartment. Imagine my surprise when *Renée* answered the phone. The moment I said I was coming home, she offered to pick me up. *Well that's that,* I thought. God had spoken. The new Mrs. Clark would be Renée.

What I didn't know was that Andrea was in the other room when Renée picked up the phone. She overheard Renée's end of the conversation and apparently felt her dear Sister was cutting in line. Andrea was having none of it. As far as she was concerned, I was hers. She literally bolted from the house and drove to the last stop the bus was scheduled to make just across the border in Louisiana. She was there waving when the bus pulled in with me on it.

I couldn't believe my eyes. Whoever said, "God works in mysterious ways," said a mouthful. I leapt from the bus and asked Andrea to marry me right there in the noise and confusion of the bus station. We were wed three months later.

Was it like I imagined it would be—serving Jehovah and the Kingdom Hall together, being helpmates, planning a family? Yes and no. We did serve together and we were helpmates. But the family was not to come for a long time.

During this period of time—the 1980s—belief was especially strong that the world would end in months or weeks or even days. Earlier in the history of the faith, Jehovah's Witnesses had been warned how unwise it would be to bring children into the world just before or during Armageddon. There would be plenty of time afterward, the literature seemed to suggest, for it implied we would live in a world that—while people were born and no one died—never became overpopulated.

That paradox aside, Andrea and I took the promise of the coming Kingdom very seriously. We refrained from having children and instead turned our energies to preaching that Kingdom.

We ended up waiting for ten years.

VIII

In With the "In" Crowd

The "Applebee's Crowd"

Marrying Andrea and taking up our faith together not only immersed us in the familial warmth of the Kingdom Hall, but it attached me to the "Applebee's crowd"—a group of Elders and favored Brothers from our congregation who socialized together after the various weekly meetings. It was a proud day for me when I was first asked to go out with this select group after one of our Theocratic Ministry meetings (see Appendix B).

While the moral teachings on such subjects as drug use, sex, and "unwholesome associations" were spelled out pretty clearly (as in, just say "no"), there were no strict prohibitions on social drinking. It was arguably a vice, and it was one that Jehovah's Witnesses were permitted to have in moderation. Perhaps because of my own problems with drinking and my wariness about revealing them, I was startled to see Brothers I'd

75

thought would never touch a beer put down three or four in one sitting while among the convivial Applebee's clique.

But surprise turned to unease and then to shock as I watched the public behavior of these men deteriorate under the influence. On one occasion, an Elder became so drunk I could tell I wasn't the only one who was uncomfortable. After repeated attempts to quiet him down, his fellow Elders grew so disconcerted by his raucous behavior that they finally "invited" him to go home. I was stunned afresh when, the next morning at the Kingdom Hall, the Elder spoke from the podium as if nothing had happened.

Though we were supposed to report the ill-behavior of our fellow Witnesses to the Elders, no one seemed willing to mention this man's behavior to his peers. No one, including me. He was an Elder, after all. That meant he had found favor in the eyes of the leadership of his Kingdom Hall, had been recommended to the guiding body of the Watchtower Society in Brooklyn, and had been appointed to his elevated station. I was merely a Brother—one who had no business throwing stones at anyone for having a few too many drinks.

Love Does Not Behave Indecently

While current Watchtower publications encourage a healthy sex life between husband and wife, their message of chastity outside of marriage—which is a positive principle in and of itself—is passed through the same filter of fear that colors many other teachings regarding such things as friendships with non-Witnesses, music, art, and literature. It created a peculiar sort of tension in the Kingdom Hall between men and women—an atmosphere of anxiety on the one hand and pleasant hyper-awareness on the other. I think this tension was aggravated by the separate and unequal roles that men and women fulfilled.

Many women among the Witnesses were nearly invisible to their own husbands, but their Field Service partners saw them always at their best—sleek, well-groomed, attractive. They were repeatedly yoked with men in circumstances that often led, in my experience, to a simmering sexual energy between Brother and Sister.

As strange as it seems, I think that energy was fed by the awareness that you were out doing the Lord's important work with this person. This made you feel important in their presence. You were at your best before them—at your strongest, sharpest, most eloquent.

This sexual tension vented itself in many insidious little ways. I saw Brothers touch and stroke women as they spoke to them—even within the sanctuary of the Kingdom Hall. I watched them back Sisters into corners to hold overly "intimate" conversations with them. I overheard sly remarks about this or that Sister's physical attributes. And I can't count the number of times I had Brothers make suggestive comments about my wife or watched as she was cornered by one or another of them in social situations.

Considering the WTS teachings on the place of women in society—especially in relation to men—it is difficult for a woman to escape these situations. At the wedding anniversary get-together that a couple from our congregation held in their home, I noticed one of the Brothers shooting glances at Andrea over his beer. I knew he was someone Andrea had done Field Service with and that she considered him a friend. Yet, at this party, she seemed to be keeping her distance.

I went over to where Andrea was standing, studiously

avoiding eye contact with her supposed friend, and said, "You should go say 'hi' to Tony, honey."

She did. He was standing by the refreshment table and she went over to get a drink and said, "Hello." He engaged her in conversation while I moved off into another circle of friends. When I glanced back at the table a few minutes later, Andrea and Tony were nowhere in sight. They were nowhere in the public rooms I searched either—together or alone. They were not in the front yard or on the back deck. Finally, I headed toward the back of the house and had hesitantly entered the hallway, when Andrea popped out of a bedroom with her friend right behind her. He was still talking.

Andrea gave me an indecipherable "look" as she passed by me, but her friend smiled, lifted his beer, and said, "We were conversing heavily on important subjects."

I could only watch him go by, wondering if there was a hidden message in those words, in that smile.

I turned on Andrea. "What happened in there?" I demanded.

"Nothing," she said, "except that he talked my ear off. But he was pushing flirtation about as far as it would go. I felt trapped in there with him—listening to him go on and on." She shook her head in frustration. "What was I supposed to do, Dan?"

She was right. What *was* she supposed to do, tell him, "Sorry, but you're boring me to tears and making me nervous, and I don't want you to think this plastic smile I'm wearing means you can touch me?" She was a woman. Her role in relation to man in the context of our faith was one of subservience. There was very little more she could do but literally "grin and bear it."

When the women were absent and liquor flowed, the Brothers would talk about them in ways that would have made them blush. They were less than apologetic about this in all-male company. Why should they apologize? Watchtower doctrine made it clear that we were incapable of having thoughts about our Sisters in faith that were anything *but* impure.

We are human, so the logic goes. This means we are fallen and are inherently sinful. The flesh is weak. Proof of this is found in the letter of the Apostle Peter to the Christian community in Rome:

I find, then, this law in my case: that when I wish to do what is right, what is bad is present with me. I really delight in the law of God according to the man I am within, but I behold in my members another law warring against the law of my mind and leading me *captive to sin's law* that is in my members. Miserable man that I am! Who will rescue me from the body undergoing this death? Thanks to God through Jesus Christ our Lord! So, then, with [my] mind I myself am a slave to God's law, but with [my] flesh to sin's law.

—Romans 7:21-25 (emphasis mine)

And it isn't even our fault—it's that old schemer Satan the Devil, the guy who tricked our first ancestors into sin and rebellion. He caused Adam and Eve to fall, and so the whole human race—every last one of us—is fallen, imperfect, sinful, immoral.

Morality isn't a choice to the inherently immoral; you can't *choose* not to sin, really, only confess your sins and muddle on. But since confession can lead to humiliation and punishment, it is a hard path, and not a popular one.

Of course, if you read on into chapter eight of Peter's letter, you might get a slightly different picture of this situation, for he goes on to say:

So, then, brothers, *we are under obligation*, not to the flesh to live in accord with the flesh; for if you live in accord with the flesh you are sure to die; but if you put the practices of the body to death by the spirit, you will live.

—Romans 8: 12, 13 (emphasis mine)

While it seems to me now that this verse discourages a fatalistic view of human nature (we're all hopelessly flawed and doomed), experience taught me that fatalism was alive and well in the Kingdom Hall.

One night after a bout of social drinking, one of the Elders—Ron—offered me a ride home. Perhaps moved by an unhealthy combination of shame and alcohol I acknowledged privately to this man that I had a problem with pornography and masturbation and intended to confess before the Elders.

He offered me this advice, "Never confess to the Elders that you have a problem with masturbation because they'll remove your privileges in the Kingdom Hall."

I vaguely recall stammering out something about duty, clearing my conscience, whatever.

Ron cut me off and said, "The best thing for you to do is to go down to Houston to get laid."

I grinned in embarrassment and said, "Are you serious? Ron, I'm *married*."

He shrugged. "Wives aren't always available, Dan. They're out doing pioneer work, they have their periods, they get pregnant. Sometimes you want something…different. I think it's a wonderful way to release this recurring sexual tension you have. You'll do better in the organization if you get that kind of stress off you."

I thought he couldn't possibly shock me any further when he proceeded to do just that. "Look, Dan. I've got a meeting of District Elders coming up in Houston in about two weeks. Why don't you drop by and pick me up afterward and we can go out and find some women."

I murmured something incoherent—at least, to my ears.

He didn't seem to hear me or notice my discomfort. "Give me a call and let me know if you want to do that," he told me.

I didn't call him. I went home in a state of shock and tried to come up with a host of creative ways I could avoid talking to him. I couldn't, of course, but I think my sudden nervousness around him warned him off. At least he didn't press the issue of our "double dating."

The kicker was that three weeks later I watched this same man speak to a Circuit Assembly of about 10,000 Jehovah's Witnesses. I don't know what the rest of the attendees took home from that assembly, but I took home a crisis of faith. I felt as if I'd just had a one-on-one with the demon Hypocrisy. I left the Circuit Assembly overwhelmed and confused, with no idea how to react or what, if anything, to do.

What I did, ultimately, was to follow my conscience. Jehovah's organization had moral rules and I had seen them broken. And by an Elder, no less. I had to speak. So I met with the Elders of my Kingdom Hall and I told them what had happened. I don't know what I expected, but it was not to be censured and told to keep my accusations to myself.

"Jehovah appointed him," said one Elder, "and Jehovah will remove him in His own due time. That's not for you to decide."

I went away even more stunned and confused than I'd
been before. I later learned that I was not the first to complain
of Ron's behavior: a group of Sisters had alleged that he'd
repeatedly touched them inappropriately. They had also been
counseled to keep silent and chastised for speaking out. No
small wonder, then, that he felt perfectly safe in speaking to me
as he'd done. He was essentially untouchable.

As I wallowed in bewilderment, I discovered that the council of Elders had told Ron I'd been to see them. Afterward, he
paid me an unwelcome visit and gave me some mystifying
advice, "Watch the movie *Quiz Show*, Dan. Pay attention to
the end."

Based on a true story, the plot of *Quiz Show* is roughly this:
An idealistic young lawyer working for a Congressional sub-
committee in the late Fifties discovers that TV quiz shows are
being fixed. He tries to expose this cheating and ends up taking the producers of one TV quiz show to court. He loses. Of
course, he is completely baffled by his loss, even as I was baffled by my "loss of face" before my Elders.

The scene Ron wanted me especially to see was the conclusion of the court case. In it, the judge sitting on the bench
finds in favor of the television show. While the young lawyer
swallows his disappointment and shock, the judge leans down
from the bench and says to the defense lawyers and their
clients, "I'll see you on the golf course tomorrow."

I got it then. I understood what Ron was trying to tell me,
what he wanted me to understand: there was a relationship
between these men that transcended law, morality, or faith.

I was torn in two at that moment. Half of Dan Clark had
started down the path of disillusionment and unwelcome discovery, but the other half—the part of me that didn't *want* to

understand—simply pulled his head back into the safe shell of the Kingdom Hall and went on with his life.

Naively, perhaps, I rejected Ron's advice about confessing my own sins. After we moved from Nacogdoches to Colorado Springs, I met with the Elders of my Kingdom Hall and told them of my recurring problems. It was just as Ron had said— I was "put on reproof," and my activities in the Hall curtailed. What this meant in practice was that I wasn't allowed to read *The Watchtower*, to participate in the Question and Answer sessions, or comment during the Book Study. I was, in a word, humiliated. While my fellow congregants didn't know what I was on reproof for, they certainly knew that I was being disciplined for something. This lasted for several months until such time as the leadership of my Kingdom Hall reckoned I could return to normal life.

I struggled with the lesson I'd learned from all of this: a Jehovah's Witness in "good standing" was not one whose behavior was good or whose sins were confessed and atoned for, but merely one whose sins were well hidden or overlooked.

IX

No Part of the World

The Running Man

Despite the challenges to my world view and the quaking of my core beliefs about who I was and who I was going through life with, I continued to strive to live as a Jehovah's Witness. I made sure my family participated in all five weekly meetings— an exhausting schedule of Book Study, Theocratic Ministry School, Meetings for Field Service, Public Talk, and Watchtower meetings. We went door-to-door on Saturdays.

I do not exaggerate when I use the word "exhausting." I have seen women go from vibrant and vital to limp and worn out trying to keep family and service apace. I've watched men—like my father—have the spring leached out of their step with every year as they tried to balance work and worship.

And the children? One would think that considering how hard I'd found the meetings as a boy, I'd have some empathy with my own children. I didn't. Strong discipline is highly regarded at meetings in the Kingdom Hall and it is a credit to any parent whose kids can sit still for two hours at a time. I certainly expected my two girls to do this. But sometimes they failed to meet those expectations.

When one of them required discipline, I'd remove her from the Hall, administer a spanking and let her cry it out in the bathroom. Then it was back to the meeting where "Dan the Good Father" received looks of approval from fellow members. That approval was what I craved. And, by God, my children would win it for me, just as they would win me polite behavior and a few extra minutes in which to deliver my message on Saturday mornings. Homeowners, I found, were less likely to be rude with a pretty little girl watching.

My daughters didn't learn about a loving God in their early years, but rather an angry, jealous God who should be feared. I was a great advertisement for this God, too, because a growing, unfocused anger got the better of me more and more often.

In an effort to burn off some of that anger, I began to run. First I just did it for exercise, health, and stress relief. Then because I found it made me feel good—runner's euphoria is quite real. Then I discovered that I was good at it and that my prowess would be rewarded. The sports letters I had failed to earn as a teenager, I was able to obtain as an adult. And I pursued them relentlessly. I ran longer and longer races until I was traveling all over the country to participate in everything from 5k meets to marathons. I pushed the envelope further and further, taking on more arduous runs that included a harrowing gallop up Pike's Peak.

And I was amply rewarded. I filled walls, shelves, and a

closet with my awards—certificates, plaques, medals. I was achieving something. I was proving myself—I had certificates that said so.

Oh, not to Andrea. Andrea never went with me to these meets, nor did she seem to care about my athletic prowess or my awards. But I wasn't doing it for Andrea. Strictly speaking, I wasn't even doing it for myself. I was trying to reach a different audience.

I didn't realize that—didn't know who I was trying to prove myself to—until my father died.

I quit running. I closed the door on the awards closet. I didn't care anymore—the one person in the world I had cared to have see those medals and certificates was gone.

Out of the Frying Pan

During my "Marathon Man" phase, I took a lot of flak from my fellow brethren and the Elders of my congregation for my unhealthy obsession with running. I was pushing too hard to excel in "the world," doing too much outside the Kingdom Hall, losing focus on what was of real importance—the work of the Watchtower Society.

After I quit running, they still had things to criticize me for, first and foremost my temper. I was an angry man, and I vented that anger on my wife, my children, and my friends in the Kingdom Hall. No one was immune; no place was too sacred. My anger was quick and violent, and running had only given it a temporary release. I was no closer to understanding where it came from, what I could do about it, or what (or whom) it was really directed at.

Then there was my work. By this point in my life, I had become an expert in the craft of restorative woodworking. I

traveled the country and the world to ply my trade. Like my
father, I was away from home for weeks at a time, but I
believed that, *unlike* my father, I was successfully balancing the
obligations of work and faith. That is, until I began to hear
gossip about "Dan and his job"—a job that had earned a lovely
home for my family and myself, nice clothing for my daughters, and a pair of BMWs for Andrea and me.

Yes, I spent a lot of time on the road. Yes, it was important
to me that I was a respected and well-paid craftsman—a craftsman whose services were called for by such prestigious clients
as the Ritz-Carlton, Omni Hotels, and high-end law firms. I
was a professional, an expert in my field, a far cry from the raw
youth who knew only how to hang drywall. Yes, I enjoyed
what I did—loved the pure, creative artistry of it. How many
of us can say that about our work—that we enjoy doing it? In
a group of people who take low-paying, low-maintenance,
often part-time jobs lest the world end while they're pursuing
a career, I'd wager there are not many. And it was mind-bog-
gling to me to come home from a business trip to be faced with
criticism from my "Brothers" for liking my job too well.

"Don't even pretend you don't like it," one of my fellow
Witnesses accused me. And the Elders exhorted me to consider
the idea that my job was interfering with my more important
work for Jehovah.

I was floored. In the past I'd quit jobs that wouldn't allow
me to go door-to-door on Saturdays, each time putting my
family in a financial bind. When I did that, I was criticized for
not being a good steward. Now I was warned that I'd never
become anything in God's earthly organization if I couldn't
keep up with the congregation average of twelve hours per
month of Field Service. Of course I was told that if I made a

larger financial contribution to the Hall—one the Elders were sure I could make out of my obviously ample resources—I would have a bigger voice in the Kingdom Hall.

A bigger voice? I didn't want a bigger voice. I wanted to be left alone to live my life. I wanted not to be made to feel guilty no matter what course of action I took. I wanted not to have this or that Brother pointed out to me as an example of those "appointed by Jehovah's Holy Spirit" with the idea that I should be like him and not like me.

Resentful? You bet. I began to think of the condemning Brothers as losers who wished they had my job. Thoughts such as these led to swift, suffocating shame which gave way, in turn, to further resentment and more anger. And, deep down inside, that other Dan—the one hiding from harsh reality—was appalled at the extreme competitiveness and lack of real love in the Kingdom Hall.

I don't know if I qualified as a legitimate "split personality" during this unsettling period of my life, but I sometimes felt like one. I no longer acknowledged my sins to anyone, least of all myself. I didn't want to think about what God knew of my private thoughts and behavior.

And yet there were lines I wouldn't or couldn't cross. I think this was because, whatever the turmoil in my heart and soul, that bewildered Dan deep within—the one with the moral and spiritual compass—occasionally spoke. It was a small voice, one I didn't always hear and sometimes ignored, but it was there.

One episode that brought this home to me with force happened during a business trip to Spain. I had gone there for a job that would take several months, and Andrea traveled with me. Our marriage wasn't at its strongest—largely because of my ambivalence and anger—and I think her occasionally coming with me on business trips was her way of trying to salvage it.

We enjoyed three months in Spain—mostly in and around Barcelona—but Andrea, who was pregnant with our second daughter, returned home to the States before I did, leaving me on my own. During my remaining month abroad, I had a chance meeting in a restaurant bar with a German girl named Britta. We talked, we "clicked," we hung out together.

Did I know what I was opening myself up to? Sure, but I had become good at hiding things from myself, and Dan of the Moral Compass merely mumbled at me in the dark.

What followed during those weeks in Spain was like something out of a Harlequin Romance novel: walks amid the Old World splendor of magnificent Barcelona and tours of the surrounding countryside; quiet, candle-lit dinners in fine restaurants, passionate and illicit embraces in quaint hotel rooms.

And there were things that were not part of your average Harlequin Romance, too—mostly drugs and booze. My new "friend" was into both. Her drug of choice was hashish. I drank and smoked with her, doping myself up to the point that I could barely hear the feeble bleating of the other Dan.

But I did hear it…a little—enough that, though we had numerous alternative kinds of sex, Britta and I never actually had intercourse.

"Why, Dan? *Why* won't you make love to me?" she asked in her thick, sexy German accent.

"Because that would be committing adultery. I can't do that."

She probably thought I was a nut case to make such a fine

distinction, but that didn't keep her from sticking with me. Until the night *I* came unstuck and pulled myself out of the bizarre relationship that was (I kept telling myself) not a relationship at all…not really.

One night in Britta's hotel room I lay on the bed all but paralyzed with alcohol and hash.

"You need to get clear," she told me. "You're not clear."

No kidding.

"What do you mean?" I asked. "How do I get clear?"

"You must take off all of your jewelry. That will clear your circuitry."

I failed to see how this would clear anything in view of all the dope I'd smoked, but Britta seemed convinced. I couldn't move, so she pulled off all my jewelry. Maybe it was the wedding ring. Maybe she thought if she could just get my wedding ring off, I'd "clear" myself of Andrea and my last reservations about committing adultery.

Whatever the reason, once she'd gotten my circuitry "clear," she sat down next to me on the bed and began to read to me…from what I belatedly realized was a book on witchcraft.

Suddenly the competitive, suspicious, political atmosphere of my Kingdom Hall seemed like the waiting embrace of a long lost mother. I broke off with the lovely witch and went home ready to rededicate myself to the aims and goals of the Kingdom Hall, to clean up my act, to *really* get clear.

Into the Fire

That's not quite how it turned out. I went home to Andrea intending to be a better husband and father. I even confessed my quasi-affair with Britta. Andrea forgave me.

But I was still confused and conflicted. I was still angry. I was still engaged in a life-or-death struggle with my own weaknesses. Serving Jehovah became harder and harder, especially going door-to-door. I never felt clean enough spiritually to engage in teaching the faith and spreading the "good news" of the Kingdom.

I looked into the faces of the people I presumed to save—the people to whom I claimed to offer the gift of eternal life and peace—and I saw, not soul-dead sinners whose lives were being frittered away on inconsequential things, but happy people, even truly joyful people, people who lived and worked and played and *loved*. People who had their lives together, who had purpose.

Visiting homes in which extended family were present—as often occurred during the holidays—the mental conflict ("cognitive dissonance" psychologists call it) was especially jarring. I saw joy and love and peace among these people as clearly as I saw their material wealth. Yet everything in the WTS literature was aimed at convincing them that they really had nothing—not *real* love, not *real* family, not *real* joy, not *real* wealth—because the truth of the world was calamity, sickness, death, disaster, and sorrow. I was supposed to convict them that their lives were empty. Vain. Impoverished. And that we—Jehovah's Witnesses—had something they should want more.

It came to me forcibly during such a visit that our ministry was "good news" only to the poorest of the poor—people who had nothing and whose only hope of riches were those promised in Heaven or in some earthly Paradise. They could have no hope of *earning* this wealth, but if they only believed a certain way—*our* way—God would make a gift of it and they'd have it without effort. To the contented individual—the individual who had put in the effort in *this* life—we could offer only that they'd be spared the coming genocide as Jehovah purged His world of the unworthy.

What was the difference, I asked myself, between having it now or having it later? The goal, in the end, was the same: material security, contentment, comfort, and ease. That was the Jehovah's Witness conception of Paradise. And it was pretty much what many people were experiencing on earth: family, happiness, beautiful homes, healthy bodies, a sense of accomplishment and spiritual fulfillment.

On Field Service days we'd sometimes talk about it as we walked back to our cars from calling at some beautiful, obviously expensive home: "Just a little while longer," one of us would say, "and *these* people will be dead. Then *we'll* occupy their beautiful homes forever."

It was a joke—or at least a half-joke. And I'd been in on the joke once. Now the thought gave me a chill.

And it raised a BIG QUESTION: *Which would I rather have, really—what these seemingly wealthy, happy people have, or the Kingdom I'm promising them…or threatening them with?*

For that matter, who was *I* to promise them this Kingdom? Who were the Jehovah's Witnesses to promise it to them? Who were we to speak of God and virtuous living?

I began to relish the time I spent away from friends, family, and faith. I liked being out of touch with all that for extended periods of time. I saw—really saw—how other people lived, how they thought, felt, and believed. I saw how they loved. The variety was endless.

Returning from one such junket, I had my own version of an "out-of-body" experience. I had just entered my neighborhood when I saw them: the Jehovah's Witnesses. I saw them as if for the first time, through a stranger's eyes, climbing out of their vans and cars, dressed in suits and ties and neat, modest dresses, tracts and Bibles tucked under their arms, breaking into teams to go door-to-door.

I had seen it all my life. I had done it countless times, and suddenly it seemed utterly alien to me.

Do I do that, too? I asked myself. *Do I look like that?* Am *I that?*

Praying not to be seen and recognized, I drove home.

The Devil You Know

So, you're wondering, why is this guy still a Jehovah's Witness? He clearly has "issues." What's keeping him there? Why doesn't he "get it" and get out?

Aside from the fear of being shunned, of losing my wife and my children, my friends and family, there is something I've observed before: *I was a Jehovah's Witness through-and-through.*

Change is hard. It can be wrenching, terrifying—like having the earth snatched out from beneath your feet. The Kingdom Hall represented security, safety, structure. As anomalous as it was, I understood it. It was familiar in every sense of the word.

In addition, the Kingdom Hall is a very closed society. We were discouraged from "knowing" much about the outside world, learning about other belief systems or schools of thought, reading any but WTS books and materials. The theology of the Kingdom Hall was all I'd known my whole life. Nothing else—not the attempt of my teachers to educate, not the catechism of the Catholic Church, not the various ideas I'd stumbled across in my adult travels—had ever had the opportunity to take root.

Of course I knew there was a world beyond the Kingdom Hall, but I didn't know how to interact with it. I didn't know its rules. It was like standing at the rim of the known world and contemplating a wild, murky place in which I already knew monsters lurked and devils played.

Hadn't I seen "devils" within my own culture? Sure. But you know what they say: *Better the devil you know than the devil you don't know.*

But what I knew—what I thought I knew—was about to change.

I had gotten in the habit when returning from one of my business trips of picking up *The Watchtower* and *Awake!* to catch up and to try get myself back into the spirit of things. Returning from a sojourn of several months, I sat down and leafed through the latest issues.

A paragraph in *Awake!* hit me like a thunderclap:

Jehovah's Witnesses firmly believe that the United Nations is going to play a major role in world events in the very near future. No doubt these developments will be very exciting. And the results will have a far-reaching impact on your life. We urge you to ask Jehovah's Witnesses in your neighborhood for more details on this matter. The Bible clearly paints a picture showing that the United Nations will very shortly be given power and authority. The UN will then do some very astonishing things that may well amaze you. And you will be thrilled to learn that there is yet a better way near at hand that will surely bring eternal peace and security!

—*Awake!* September 1991

I felt as if all the blood had drained out of my body. I read the passage again—surely I'd misread it. It seemed to be saying that not only would the United Nations do some "exciting"

things in the future, but that the Jehovah's Witnesses were an
authority on the organization.

It took me a couple readings to realize that it was double-
talk. We'd *always* believed the UN would play "a major role in
world events in the very near future"—it was the "disgusting
thing" spoken of in the Book of Daniel that was "standing in
the holy place." Of course the Bible said it would shortly be
given "power and authority" and do "astonishing things"—it
was the "scarlet-colored beast" of the book of Revelations!
What could be more astonishing than that metaphorical
beast's support of false religion or its attempt to usurp the purpose of the Kingdom of God?

But why the suddenly veiled language? The WTS had
never been shy about proclaiming that the UN was an "anti-
Christ" organization, man's arrogant attempt to bring about
peace on earth, or that it was disgusting, evil, and demonic.

Deep down inside, the hidden Dan had begun to quake.
He trembled harder with every successive mention the WTS
tracts made of the UN. They cited the UNICEF publication
The State of the World's Children 1991 and supported its con-
clusions about the importance of educating girls and women.
In fact, they cited any number of UN-sponsored programs and
reports on humanitarian issues, seeming to praise the hard
work of organizations such as UNICEF and the World Health
Organization (WHO) in their efforts to improve the lot of
children worldwide.

I suppose it should not have shocked me when it was revealed
that, in 1991, the Watchtower Bible and Tract Society had
applied and been accepted for status as a Non-Governmental
Organization (NGO) with the UN, a role it shares with a variety
of secular bodies and other religious groups.

The following is a mere sampling of the religious organizations that share UN NGO status—these are all groups the Watchtower Society considers representatives of "false" religion.

- World Jewish Congress
- International Association of Friends (Quakers)
- International Catholic Association for Radio and Television
- Anglican Consultative Council
- Franciscans International
- Jesuit Refugee Service
- Lutheran World Federation
- Seventh-Day Adventists
- World Council of Independent Christian Churches
- World Muslim Congress
- International Buddhist Relief Organization
- Brahma Kumaris World Spiritual University
- Federation of Zoroastrian Associations of North America
- Interfaith International

The change in language I'd seen in the publications now made perfect sense. In order to become an NGO the WTS had to meet certain criteria set forth by the United Nations:

- Mobilizing public opinion in support of the UN
- Disseminating information about the UN to their membership
- Promoting UN observances and international years
- Promoting knowledge of UN principles and activities

The Watchtower Society had been using its own publications—publications I had believed to be Jehovah-God's channel of communication with His people—to do these things, in metaphorical terms, to carry out the agenda of the "scarlet-colored beast."

I said I should not have been shocked by this, but I was. Deeply. Not only was I quaking inside, but the solid earth of Watchtower doctrine had just quivered beneath my feet.

Ah, you may be thinking, *that's* when you left.

But no, not yet—perhaps because I needed help.

And help was about to arrive.

X

A Bite of the Apple

God Sheds More Light

The Watchtower Society's seeming acceptance of the UN was just the beginning. Every time I opened a *Watchtower* or *Awake!* now I was blindsided by articles that warped the very foundation of my belief and left me breathless.

What was happening? The publications tried to answer this by noting that "Jehovah shed new light" on certain issues allowing His organization on earth to have "a clearer idea" of His intentions. This meant that the Watchtower Society had a "clearer idea" of God's view of the United Nations in 1991 when it applied to it for Non-Governmental Organization status than it did three years earlier when the 1988 edition of *Revelation, Its Grand Climax at Hand* referred to it as "a blasphemous counterfeit of God's Messianic Kingdom." It had a "clearer idea" of how God felt about voting in 1999 when it became a matter of individual conscience than it did in 1970 when Jehovah's Witnesses in the Cameroon were imprisoned and tortured rather than being issued a voting registration card.

And even as I watched, it got a "clearer idea" of the 1914 generation prophecy that had, up until then, assured us that the world would end and Armageddon would come by the end of the 1990s.

If you'll recall, this prophecy stated that:

…Jesus said: 'This generation will by no means pass away until all these things occur [including the end of this system].' Which generation did Jesus mean? He meant *the generation of people who were living in 1914*. Those persons yet remaining of that generation are now very old. However, some of them will still be alive to see the end of this wicked system. *So of this we can be certain*: Shortly now there will be a sudden end to all wickedness and wicked people at Armageddon.

—*You Can Live Forever In Paradise On Earth*, 1982
(emphasis mine)

In 1995, this changed. Jehovah's new light illumined this prophecy so much that the Watchtower Society was inspired to change its meaning. The November 1995 *Watchtower* said of Jesus' prophecy about "this generation" that it "apparently refers to the peoples of earth (now) who see the signs of Christ's presence but fail to mend their ways."

The Great Clock had stopped ticking.

After 130 plus years of urgent preaching about the impending end of the world, the Watchtower Society had reinterpreted the prophecy in such a way that there was no end in sight. I certainly couldn't imagine that the world would ever be free of a "generation" of people "who see the signs of Christ's presence, but fail to mend their ways." That "generation" had already endured since the time of Jesus.

Perhaps you, the reader, can't grasp what this meant to someone who had lived an entire life with the idea that the end was near. Let me see if I can help you imagine it.

From childhood you forego things other kids take for granted. Your education is an afterthought (many Jehovah's Witness children of my mother's generation were removed from school before completing their education); you are forbidden to participate in sports and are expected to avoid association with non-Witnesses; you are encouraged to view your non-Witness friends as evil, sinful, doomed. As a teen you reject an advanced education and career training because to do so would be a futile waste of time. As an adult you may forego having a family, a career or even a full-time job because time is so short that all your energy must go toward pioneering.

As a result of this belief in the end of the world I stepped into adulthood practically illiterate, with no real skills, no goals, no purpose beyond trumpeting the end of the world. In the absence of that purpose I had none. It was the ultimate irony: In my youth I had been without purpose because I had strayed from the beliefs that had defined my life to that point. As an adult I found myself in the same position because those beliefs had been redefined. And were it not for the grace of God I would *still* have been a functionally illiterate, unskilled man—a man prepared for the end of the world, but completely *unprepared* for it to continue.

A new light? A clearer idea?

No, I thought, *Jehovah has not shed a new light. They've changed the prophecy!*

This altered the practical aspects of our entry into the

coming Kingdom as well. When "this generation" had applied to the folks around in 1914, the faithful flock was to be led through Armageddon and the Tribulation by members of that self-same generation. The new "clearer idea" taught that those who were Elders at the time of the End would be elevated to "princes" and would guide the faithful through the coming chaos and into the Kingdom of God on earth.

Yes, the same Elders who drank to excess, who talked casually about easy sex, who leered at each other's wives, then judged their brethren for their secret conduct—*these* were the "princes" destined to lead Jehovah's people into Paradise.

Not long after this I had the Saturday pioneering meltdown that I described in the first chapter of this book. Only recently have I thought about what effect that angry outburst may have had on my wife, Andrea. At the time I was only aware of my own secret crisis.

Know Your Worth

Around this time I also began having some "issues" in my work life. A fellow I was subcontracting with to do some finish work on a residence stiffed me for $150 that was due me. After unsuccessful attempts to get him to pay me, my reaction was to simply stop working. I didn't hear from the contractor, but I did hear from his client, a woman named Martha.

She called me up one day and said, "Dan, where are you? I have more work that needs doing."

I explained the situation to her—that the contractor she'd hired had refused to pay me what he owed—and was quick to assure her that I wasn't going to try to collect from her.

Her response was, "Well, come on over. I'll hire you and pay you directly."

The job, she explained, was to do the same refinishing on the woodwork in her son's house (right next door to hers, as it turned out) she'd had done on hers. She asked what I'd charge for that.

"I'd charge $800, same as for your work," I told her.

"Deal," she said. "I've got a check for you. Drop by my son's house and I'll give it to you."

At her son Benjamin's house I got out of my truck and looked up the street to see this imposing figure striding toward me. The woman in the black dress with the flamboyant red and white scarf seemed much taller than she really was. She carried herself with such dignity and confidence that she drew my gaze like a magnet. Did I say "imposing?" "Intimidating" would be more accurate. This was a woman who, if she walked down a crowded street, would impel the crowd to part in front of her in acknowledgement of her sheer sense of authority.

I was frozen to the sidewalk. She was looking right at me—or perhaps through me—with a wide smile on her lips.

"Hi. You must be Dan," she said, holding out her hand. "I'm Martha."

I shook her hand and acknowledged that I was Dan three times in quick succession, I was so nervous in her overwhelming presence.

She offered me a check. "This is for the damages you incurred from my contractor."

I opened my mouth to object that *she* didn't owe me the money, *he* did, but my eyes had fallen on the amount. It was twice what the contractor owed me. I glanced up at her, but she only smiled more deeply and said, "I look forward to working with you."

When I finished the doors in her son's home, she asked me to drop by her place to collect my check.

She greeted me as if I were a long lost friend. "Hi, Dan!" she said, and I stammered out my hellos like a hopelessly bashful schoolboy. "Have a seat," she told me and waved me to a chair in a roomful of fabulous hand-crafted and hand-painted furniture.

The entire home was absolutely gorgeous; its uncluttered rooms contained the most tasteful and elegant furnishings. In fact the furniture was what we talked about. I commented on how well-made and beautiful it was.

Martha smiled at me and said, "I would like you to refinish all the furniture in this house."

I was stunned and positive I couldn't have heard her right. "But it's already finished," I protested. "What do you want *me* to do?"

"Oh, just do that thing you do to furniture—you know, beat it up, antique it, glaze it. Whatever it is you do, do it to my furniture. Make it more beautiful!"

I was terrified. The pieces were so obviously expensive and of the highest quality of workmanship, yet she acted as if she'd picked them up at a garage sale. I can't begin to describe how nervous I was.

I came over very early the next morning to pick up a load of furniture. I worked on it all day and brought the first load back to her the very same evening, afraid to even have such things in my workshop overnight—my God, what if someone broke in and stole them, or the place burned down?

"What do I owe you?" she asked when I'd unloaded the last piece.

I did a quick calculation: She'd paid me an extra $150 on

the first job I'd done for her, so I told her a couple of hundred would be sufficient.

She laughed at me. "Come on, Dan. It's more than that, and you know it. Tell me what you're worth."

"Let me think about it," I said, and drove home to get a few more pieces of furniture.

I'd no sooner arrived back at Martha's house than she asked again, "How much do I owe you?"

I stammered and stuttered and finally came up with, "I don't know…$500?"

She gave me a stern look and said, "Dan, don't cheat yourself like that. When you bring my last piece to me, tell me what I owe you and *don't cheat yourself.* Your time is worth more than that. *You're* worth more than that."

So, when I brought the last piece, I conjured every bit of courage in my body to tell her that the job was really worth (gasp!) $950.

She laughed out loud and said, "You're *still* cheating yourself!"

I laughed too—nervously—put up my hands and said, "I can't take anymore, Martha, really."

"Okay," she said, "can you take a tip?"

Oh, give up, Dan, I thought, and nodded.

She grinned at me. "Good! I'll go get your check."

She came back and handed me a check for $1,500. I couldn't believe my eyes. I started to protest, to refuse to take the money, but she pointed at me and said firmly, "Know your worth."

Know my worth? What a novel concept. It was not something I had ever been encouraged to do—at least not in a positive sense. My "worth" as a Jehovah's Witness had been

bound to what I was willing to do for or sacrifice for the organization. My inherent worth—the worth of any human
being—was zero. In fact, it could only be expressed in negative
numbers because any and every human being was sinful,
fallen, less than nothing.

I *had* no worth. None of us did.

But I didn't say that. Not to Martha. I had the feeling it
wouldn't be well-received.

I think she was reading my face or my mind, though,
because she said, "I have a personal question I'd like to ask you."

Perhaps feeling a bit warmed by this confident woman's
sense of my value, I said, "Sure. What is it?"

"You're a Jehovah's Witness aren't you?"

I could only stare at her. How in God's name could she
possibly know that? I'd certainly never mentioned it to her. I
reluctantly admitted that I was, indeed, a Jehovah's Witness.
"How did you know?" I asked.

"Well, you all act the same—kind of goofy," she joked.
"Don't worry. I love Jehovah's Witnesses. In fact, I've helped
many JW's in my neighborhood."

"Helped?" I repeated. "How so?" The Witnesses I knew
were unlikely to accept any kind of help from an outsider—
especially such a brash one.

"I take in kids that have been shunned or rejected by their
families. I let them stay with me until they can get on their
feet. There's some recovery time there."

Recovery time. I didn't doubt it.

Quite suddenly I felt as if I could tell this woman *anything*
about myself and have her understand. Without considering
the consequences, I opened my mouth and said, "I think I
need some help."

I was to need it sooner than I'd thought.

The same evening Martha counseled me to know my worth, she told me that she'd prayed to God that *very* morning to make her available to someone who needed her help. I was, I guess you could say, an answer to her prayers. She was most certainly an answer to mine—prayers I didn't even know I was sending heavenward.

She also said that if I were to accept her help I needed to give her 100 percent. "I need you to be here when you say you're going to, and do what we agree to do. I want you to know that whatever you need, I'm here for you, and whatever subject you bring to me, we'll work on it."

I was soon to bring her a subject—the changes that the Watchtower Society had been making in its doctrine during my lifetime. Everything from prophecy about the end times, to voting, to the UN. I also timidly admitted to her that I had developed an interest in some very questionable reading material from a WTS point-of-view—the works of Dr. Wayne Dyer (affectionately known as "the father of motivation" among his fans) and Dr. Deepak Chopra, a leader of thought about the connection between health and spirituality.

Martha almost fell over in disbelief. "Witnesses aren't allowed to read those books."

"Yeah," I said, shame-faced, "but I'm drawn to them for some reason."

Martha's smile was beatific. We were, she told me, a match made in heaven. So, she became my "enabler," introducing me to new ideas, new philosophies, new ways of looking at the world—feeding my hunger for these things. We began our work on co-dependency, sexual addition, and alcoholism. I learned about philosophies as diverse as Science of Mind, the

Course in Miracles, and the Enneagram. Whatever I was interested in, she'd research it and we'd look into it, sometimes joined by her son, Benjamin, and her husband, Gerald.

She also helped me clarify my confused feelings about the Watchtower Society and its teachings, bringing me a historical perspective I'd been lacking before.

From Crime to Conscience

It was Martha who inadvertently lit the fuse on a bomb that had been planted at home. One day she brought me some information she'd found online about the "new light" shed on the Watchtower teachings regarding blood transfusions and organ transplants.

From the teaching I'd grown up with—"Whether whole or fractional, one's own or someone else's, transfused or injected, it [transfusion] is wrong."—the WTS had come to view transfusions (like voting) as a matter of conscience. According to the August 1, 1995 *Watchtower,* "...the Center for Bloodless Surgery utilizes alternatives to blood transfusions, including *the reinfusion of a patient's own blood*—a technique that some Witnesses may find unobjectionable under certain circumstances."

Not only that, but a believer might have a transfusion of some *components* of blood such as globulin, clotting agents, and plasma proteins. Taking all of the individual components the WTS would now allow believers to "consume" as a whole, Witnesses could technically make use of somewhere upwards of 97 percent of the blood. Organ transplants too, which at one point were regarded as "cannibalism" according to several issues of *The Watchtower*, were no longer absolutely unacceptable.

It was stunning, but I was already pretty punch-drunk.

Still, I was floored when Martha showed me a developing story out of Colombia where the Watchtower Society had recently suspended its ban on transfusions after the Constitutional Court issued a declaration against it.

"This," stated Court President Vladmiro Naranjo, "is a form of murder, moreover, first degree murder… Religious freedom is not absolute, there are limitations. A religion that attempts to claim the life of a person cannot be legally permitted." The story included the information that, at a time Colombian (and indeed American) believers were being disfellowshipped for the same offense, the WTS had already guaranteed to the European Commission on Human Rights that there would not be any sanctions levied against Witnesses in the Commission's jurisdiction who accepted blood transfusions for themselves or their children.

"I wonder what Andrea would think of this," I said.

"Don't show it to Andrea," Martha advised me. "I think it would blow her out of the water."

I didn't listen, of course. I took the information home and showed Andrea that blood transfusions had gone from being a reason for disfellowshipping to a matter of conscience.

Andrea's reaction was swift and extreme. "They lied to us!" she told me. "They're liars! First they say it's a crime against God, then they say it's a matter of conscience? How can they *do* that?"

I tried to calm her down, mumbling about "a new light" and "a clearer idea," but when she finally did calm down, her stone-cold silence was worse than her raw fury. She closed down and withdrew into herself. The next thing I new she had submitted her letter of resignation to the Kingdom Hall and had arranged an "exit interview" with three Elders.

Up to this point, I'd had no idea that my wife was at all uneasy in the Kingdom Hall. Why did this particular straw break the camel's back? It wasn't until much later that she explained it to me. When I'd shown Andrea the documentation Martha had tracked down, the first thought that crossed her mind was, *What if one of our girls had needed a blood transfusion or organ transplant six months ago—or even six weeks ago? She might have died then. I might have let my baby die for what someone decided is now a matter of conscience.*

I can't fault either her reasoning or her emotions. She surely saw the cover of the May 22, 1994 *Awake!* magazine, which showed photos of twenty-six children who had died because they and/or their parents believed the "truth" of the Watchtower Society's absolute position on the sinfulness of blood transfusions and organ transplants. The congratulatory title of that issue was "Youths Who Put God First." One year later, the truth was apparently not quite so absolute. One year later, they might not have died.

Something else had been troubling Andrea, too. This was the Watchtower doctrine on sexual abuse and rape. The basic doctrine called for a charge of abuse or rape to be validated by two witnesses or a confession by the alleged perpetrator. It also called for the victim to have resisted the attack. Sexual predators don't normally choose public places for their crimes, so the idea of having to have witnesses struck Andrea as absurd, but it was the definition of "resistance" that disturbed her the most.

Before January of 1964, rape was considered "willful fornication" and a reason for disfellowshipping if the victim didn't scream. In January of that year, the WTS determined that screaming was not necessary to validate a claim of rape. But in

1969, a woman could once again be disfellowshipped if she reported a rape, but admitted she didn't scream. This continued to go back and forth over the years, and though I didn't notice it, Andrea certainly did. This uncertainty was appalling enough in her eyes, but even worse was the idea that these things were being decided by a group of men, who would also decide whether the criteria had been met to "prove" a rape had occurred.

Andrea's internal conflict over both these issues was now at a full boil, though I still had little inkling of this. And though still battling my own demons, I wanted to show solidarity with my wife. I offered to go with her to her meeting with the Elders, but she refused.

"I have to do this on my own," she told me.

I understood. And so I put our daughters to bed and sat at home and waited for her to come back.

When she finally came through the door hours later, she was in tears—emotionally drained. "They shamed me," she said. "They said I was Eve—wicked and weak. They said I'd 'taken a bite of the apple.'"

She dragged herself to bed after that, exhausted and emptied out. But the next morning Andrea Clark was a different woman—happy and free.

I was neither of those things.

XI

A Clearer Idea

The Parable

The fallout from Andrea's disassociation from the Witnesses was immediate. The Elders were angry. And they found the perfect target for their anger: me. They held that Andrea's defection was my fault. I was a poor steward of my family, a weak head-of-household. I hadn't been holding regular home Bible studies, I'd slacked off on pioneering, I'd neglected to keep an eye on what was going on in my own home. I had allowed the world into my domain—into Jehovah's domain.

And Andrea? She was worse than Eve, she was a Jezebel. Irredeemable. Lost. But far from being demoralized by severing herself from the Kingdom Hall, she seemed to flourish. She was considering going back to school; she was investigating other spiritual paths.

"Your wife has not only taken a bite of the apple," one

Elder told me, "but she's keeping it in the refrigerator so she can continue to eat it."

When the condemnation had died down a bit, though, they turned their attention to my future. Even the friends I had within the Kingdom Hall treated this as if it were a divorce. As far as they were concerned, Andrea was out of the picture. And to hear them tell it, they'd known all along she wasn't any good.

"Don't worry," said one friend, "there are plenty of good Sisters in the truth."

I was stunned to feeble silence: they were already planning my next marriage!

Now you might suppose that someone who removed themselves willingly from the Kingdom Hall would simply be treated like any other non-Witness. You wouldn't go out of your way to either cultivate their company or avoid it. You would simply be neutral—friendly, but not intimate, per-haps—in the hope that they would one day wish to return to the fold.

Not so. When a Jehovah's Witness leaves or is asked to leave the Watchtower Society through disfellowshipping, that person is shunned. This doesn't mean they can't attend public meetings, but it does mean that they will not be spoken to or greeted when they do. Their former friends and colleagues will no longer socialize with them.

Since I was married to her, I wasn't expected to shun Andrea, nor were our daughters. But we were not to discuss spiritual issues with her, and I was to discourage her from tak-ing a role in our little girls' spiritual training.

In Andrea's case, the shunning was so complete that even our Jehovah's Witness neighbors reacted to the news of her defection. I watched from the kitchen window one afternoon as Andrea went out to do some gardening in the back yard. The family living in the house behind us—also Witnesses— were out in their yard when she exited the back door with her gardening gear. She waved at them. They abandoned what they were doing and shooed their kids into the house, closing the door firmly behind them.

Even more hurtful, though, was the behavior of people who had known—and presumably loved—Andrea for years. They avoided her, turned away from her when they saw her in public, and refused to visit our home. And yet my fellows at the Kingdom Hall still expected *me* to socialize with them— alone. The real impact of this hit me when, early in the process, a couple of the Brothers and their wives invited me out to dinner with them after a meeting.

"Sure," I said. "Just let me go home and get Andrea and the girls."

"Dan," they said, "you know Andrea can't come. She's severed herself from Jehovah's organization."

This brought me up short. Was this the way you treated someone you wanted back in your family? I thought of the parable of the Prodigal Son whose father is so happy to see him return that he races to embrace him, though he smells of pigs. He goes further and makes a feast for him to welcome him home. He forgives him utterly for having caused the family distress. And to the sibling who complains that he has been faithful all these years and received no such treatment, the father replies: "Child, you have always been with me, and all the things that are mine are yours; but we just had to enjoy ourselves and rejoice, because this your brother was dead and came to life, and he was lost and was found." (Luke 15:31,32)

This parable of Christ resonated so strongly with me that I had to wonder: where was this spirit of love and reconciliation in God's visible organization? Translated back into parable, the treatment Andrea—and all other disassociated believers—received was tantamount to being booted from the house for even asking to leave and then left to starve in the barnyard. Where was the spirit of Christ in *that* scenario? Moreover, who'd want to return to a household that was that cold and unloving? Would the Prodigal Son have run to a father whose arms were folded across his breast and whose eyes blazed at him in cold fury? I didn't think so.

I tried to imagine Andrea doing it—returning to the Kingdom Hall and begging to be let back in. I tried to imagine her spending six months to a year attending meetings at which no one would speak to her, smile at her, embrace her. Sneaking in late and leaving early so as to avoid contact with the faithful sons and daughters of Jehovah. Suffering the humiliation of having to request reinstatement not once, but twice or more—for it was inevitable that the request would be rejected at least once.

Once upon a time, when I was a kid, a person who had been through this process was at least welcomed back warmly—their reinstatement announced and applauded. Now, Andrea's best hope was to slide inconspicuously back into line and work at rebuilding her life in the Kingdom Hall—if she were to ever want such a life again. And that, I couldn't imagine. I couldn't imagine my wife or anyone else wanting to come home to humiliation so complete. Yet statistics indicate that about one-third of disfellowshipped Witnesses go through this agonizing process to return to an organization that truly seems not to want them.

That was the impression I had, at any rate—that they were not wanted. No, it was more than an impression. I was certain that those Brothers in Brooklyn—the ones presiding over the Watchtower Society—didn't want their prodigal sons and daughters back. Ever. It was Martha who helped clarify this for me. Martha who, with her son, Benjamin, involved me in a little role-playing game during one of my sessions with them. They acted out the parable of the Prodigal Son and, as I watched a smiling Martha enfold her own son in a loving embrace, all the paradoxes I'd ever encountered in the Kingdom Hall collided in my head and heart.

I left that session with The Question pressing at my lips and arranged to meet with the Elders of my congregation. I shared with them the parable of the Prodigal Son. I asked The Question: "Why don't we welcome people back with open arms as the father does in the parable?"

Their reply: "Because, like the Prodigal Son, these people—people like your wife—should never have roamed. This is where they always should have been—in Jehovah's earthly organization. Why should we applaud them for simply doing what they should have done in the first place—remain faithful?"

It was, I realized, the elder brother's argument. The one the father (that is to say, the Lord) refutes when He says, "...all the things that are mine are yours, but we just had to...rejoice, because this your brother...was lost and was found."

The Prodigal

"Why do you still believe?"

I've no doubt the reader is wondering this. I know Martha was. Hell, *I* was.

The answers are woven into the pages of this book. I was raised with it. It was the framework of my life even at times when I was not aware of the fact—even when I was not a practicing Witness. It was all I knew. All other faiths, I had been taught, were summed up in the inerrant scripture as "false religion."

And then, there was the fear: by rejecting this faith—the only faith I really knew anything about—was I not rejecting God, Himself?

I posed that question, at least indirectly, to Martha.

"Why do you think you'd be rejecting God?" she wondered.

"Because the Watchtower Society is the 'faithful and discreet slave' that gives out the spiritual food of Jehovah," I answered.

"Is it? Or does it merely claim to be?"

I wriggled uncomfortably. "Okay. It claims to be."

"And what evidence does it offer?"

"The Bible prophecies."

Ah, yes. The Bible prophecies. There is at least one entire book in the Watchtower Society library dedicated to that subject, but Martha seemed less than impressed with the organization's track record. She reminded me of that now, pointing out all the missed prophecies about the time of the end and how the WTS had later tried to step away from the human consequences of those prophecies, claiming they were "never inspired, never perfect."

"And what about the changes they've made in doctrine over the years?" she asked me. "That seems to bother you a great deal."

I shrugged. "Well, yes, but…well, maybe they're right. Maybe God is just shedding more light on these things."

She did something completely unexpected at that point.

She called to Benjamin, who entered from the next room with a wagon filled with Bibles. Twenty-five slightly different translations of the Bible as it happened. One of them was the Watchtower's own New World Translation.

"Read to me," Martha said, holding out the Watchtower Bible. "Read to me about the blood."

Puzzled, I turned to the key verse upon which the Watchtower doctrine regarding blood transfusions is based: Acts 15:29. I read, "…to keep abstaining from things sacrificed to idols and from blood… If you carefully keep yourselves from these things, you will prosper. Good health to you!"

"What has the 'faithful and discreet slave' said that means?" Martha asked.

"That we should not take blood in any form." I did not want to confront, at that moment, the fact that the WTS had since said that perhaps some forms of blood were okay, or at least "unobjectionable." "Further, if we refuse to take blood we will have good heath."

"Because the apostle says, 'Good health to you?'"

I nodded. "We've taught that door-to-door, actually. People often ask us about that. We made a point of showing them that the apostles recognized the health consequences."

"'Good health to you,'" repeated Martha. "That sounds like a farewell phrase to me—like the closing of a letter."

"No," I argued. "It's part of the verse."

Martha picked up the King James Version of the Bible and read, "That ye abstain from meats offered to idols, and from blood…from which if ye keep yourselves, ye shall do well. *Fare ye well.*"

"What?" I said stupidly. Then, "But the King James Version was created to be elegant, not accurate."

"Okay," Martha conceded. She picked up another Bible—the New International Version. This translation had been put together by a committee of Jewish and Christian scholars from a variety of denominations with accuracy at the center of the mandate. This one read, "You are to abstain from food sacrificed to idols, from blood.... You will do well to avoid these things. Farewell."

Benjamin next read from the New American Standard Bible: "...that you abstain from things sacrificed to idols and from blood...if you keep yourselves free from such things, you will do well. Farewell."

The Contemporary English translation rendered the passage about blood: "You should not eat any meat that *still has the blood in it...*" and the closing phrase as, "We send our best wishes," but it agreed about the nature of that closing phrase.

So did all the other Bibles—every last one. The Amplified Bible added the parenthetical words, "be strong."

Indeed.

I needed to be strong at that point, because I had just remembered a Circuit Assembly in 1980—just after I first reattached myself to the Kingdom Hall—at which the believers were instructed to stop using this passage in Acts to support the health consequences of blood transfusions. I said as much to Martha and Benjamin.

"What does that suggest to you?" Martha asked. "That this scripture everyone thought supported the teaching on transfusions suddenly didn't anymore?"

"God shed more light so we'd have a clearer idea," I stammered, falling back on the party line.

Martha leaned toward me, a Bible still in her hands. "Did

He?" she asked. "Is this a clearer idea…or an entirely new idea? And if it's an entirely new one, where did it come from?"

"From the faithful and discreet slave. They give the guidance from the Lord as it's illumined for them and as the congregation needs it."

"And that explains why you left high school with no plans for higher education? Why you piddled around for half your life in dead-end jobs with no skills? Why you and Andrea waited ten years to have kids? Why Andrea won't be celebrated like the Prodigal Son if she decides to go back to the Kingdom Hall? Why a child that died for lack of a transfusion last year would still be alive if only they'd been able to hold out until God shed more light on the scripture?"

Her words scalded me. "But the Bible is inerrant," I argued. "And Jehovah's organization…"

Was clearly not.

I sat, stunned at my own epiphany. They'd said it themselves in the chaotic days of 1979 that saw the disfellowshipping of so many Witnesses: "In this regard, however, it must be observed that this 'faithful and discreet slave' was never inspired, never perfect."

And if this was true—if they were not inspired, not perfect in their understanding of the scripture, then how could their word be accorded so much power? How could they presume to control the lives and condition the faith of so many?

How could they claim the authority to decide what doctrine led to salvation when their understanding of that doctrine was imperfect?

"Where does it come from, Dan?" Martha asked me now. "Where does that information come from that the Watchtower Society gives you?"

"They say it comes from Jesus Christ to give us our spiritual food at the proper time," I answered.

"So, all your instruction, guidance, and direction for life comes through this organization—the Watchtower Bible and Tract Society in Brooklyn, New York."

I nodded.

"Well, what if they told you that brown was Jehovah's color and that everyone could only wear brown?"

I laughed. It felt good to laugh at that moment, and I mistakenly thought she was letting me off the hook. "They wouldn't do that."

"But what if they did, Dan? They've already legislated on much more important things than what color suit you wear."

"I guess I'd wear brown," I said. "But why would they dictate that?"

"Why would they legislate on some of the other issues they have?" she asked.

"Well, the scriptures…" I started to explain, then realized I was right back in the Catch 22 I'd found myself in a moment before.

The Watchtower interpretation of any number of scriptural passages had been "imperfect" before, yet they'd felt at the time they issued those interpretations, and based doctrine on them, that they were the absolute truth. They clearly believed they'd been accorded the authority to interpret scripture—regardless of the fact that their interpretations changed…and scripture didn't.

"Where do those rules come from, Dan?" Martha asked me again.

"They come from the Lord."

"How? Does the Lord speak directly to the leaders of the faith in Brooklyn?"

I'd never heard them claim that. "No. Even what Charles Taze Russell wrote wasn't inspired."

"Then how can it come from the Lord, Dan? If it did come from the Lord, wouldn't it be inspired? Wouldn't it be perfect? And if it's not, how can you give your entire life over to it?"

"But the *Bible* is inspired," I argued.

"All right. But then why not just read it for yourself and decide how to live your life?"

"I can't. I don't understand that stuff. I don't have the authority to interpret scripture."

"Then who gave *them* the authority to do it?"

I shook my head. I didn't know. I suppose it was a question I'd never really asked. I'd just accepted that the leaders of the Watchtower Society had the authority to interpret scripture, not just for themselves, but everybody.

"And what if the Watchtower Society decided tomorrow that they were going to shut down?" Martha asked me. "What if they admitted that they never could see the future, that they'd made too many erroneous prophecies, that they weren't sure about blood or organ transplants, or when Armageddon started, or even that God insisted on being called 'Jehovah.' What if there was going to be *no more Watchtower Society?* What would you do? More to the point—what would you *be?*"

Terror gripped me. I couldn't even *think* such a thing. The very hint of that thought opened a huge chasm of unknown depth under my feet.

It hit me like a lightning strike: *I had no personal relationship with God.*

Apart from slavishly carrying out the mandates of the Kingdom Hall and meeting its criteria for Godliness, I had no spiritual life—no essential value—whatsoever. Remove me from that context and there would be nothing left. *I am made up of this organization,* I thought. *I'm nothing without this organization.*

I quickly evaded Martha's perceptive gaze and changed the subject.

But the questions were out in the open; I could no longer stuff them away where I couldn't see them. If there was light being shed, it was being shed on the paradoxes and contradictions I had lived with my entire life.

But light was also being shed on my own spiritual bankruptcy. The truth was, I had grown up in this box. It was my box—familiar and safe—and I was used to defining myself in relation to it. I knew no other way to define Dan Clark. But I had come to realize it was also a filter. It literally stood between me and God. In fact, I knew God only through the demoralized Sisters, the lecherous Brothers, the wrathful and hypocritical Elders, the changing "truths" of the Watchtower Society.

It was with all these things percolating in my mind that I went to my next meeting at the Kingdom Hall. I opened the door into the sanctuary and peered in. Up near the podium, a group of Brothers murmured among themselves. I caught the tenor of their mirthful conversation—they were gossiping, laughing scornfully at someone. For all I knew, it might have been me.

The collective outrage of decades rolled over me in a great, breaking wave. *I'm done with this,* I thought, turned on my heel, and left.

I tendered my letter of resignation immediately. Recalling Andrea's experience, I expected someone to contact me to arrange a meeting with the Elders. I was ready for it. I was ready for them.

But no one from the Kingdom Hall ever did contact me. They simply let me go.

XII

Afterlife/Life After

Heaven to Hell in Sixty Seconds Flat

Leaving the Kingdom Hall seemed to open a door to a whole new room in my life. With my time no longer going into ministerial work, I joined Andrea in going back to school. I concentrated on doing a good job at work. I tried to give more attention to my marriage and to my family. I finally had to face my drinking problem, where before I had only edged carefully around it.

Martha had long hinted at me that I should confront my relationship with alcohol, but I wasn't ready. I reacted to her hints with resentment, suspecting that she and Andrea were talking behind my back.

I became ready the day I left a bar in Loveland, cheerfully drunk, and took a walk up the street. The day seemed extraordinarily beautiful to me and I became fascinated by the way little birds flew up from the sidewalk before me as if heralding my passage. It reminded me, suddenly and forcefully, of my time in Barcelona, where the pigeons would lift from the plazas like a living cloud as I crossed the aged flagstones.

I was smitten with the day, with the moment. I was content, peaceful, even happy.

Then I bumped into a man walking in the opposite direction. He said something sharp to me—maybe only, "Watch where you're going." I don't recall. I only recall going off on him like a bad firecracker. He kept moving and I stumbled on up the street, no longer content with the world.

A girl sitting on a brick wall along the sidewalk began to call to me incoherently (or perhaps I was *hearing* incoherently). Something about needing a car part—an alternator or some such nonsense.

I looked at her sitting there and thought, *What if I were to yank you off that wall and toss you into traffic, bitch?*

And there I froze. Was this the same guy who, mere moments before, had been mesmerized by the beauty of small birds and sunlight? How had I gone so quickly from Heaven to Hell?

I went immediately to Martha and asked her.

"You have a drinking problem, Dan. You have since you were a teenager." She paused and looked at me shrewdly. "Haven't you?"

I had, and I knew it, but I was acting out a classic denial scenario, my fickle memory shielding me from recollections of my first high school drinking binge with Wade. That time I'd been in the Heaven of Snow instead of the Heaven of Small Birds, but the pattern was the same. Heaven to Hell in sixty seconds flat.

"I'm not an alcoholic," I protested now. "I'm *not*."

Martha's gaze grew sharper. "My husband, Gerald is a recovering alcoholic, you know."

I was flabbergasted. "You're kidding. He can't be." I couldn't feature it: a successful anesthesiologist—a nice, Santa Claus of a guy like Gerald, an alcoholic?

I didn't admit my problem just then, but Gerald did confirm what Martha had said about him and invited me to an Alcoholics Anonymous meeting so I could see how he was dealing with his problem.

Maybe halfway through the meeting, as the people told their stories, I realized I saw myself reflected in all of them. Their stories were my story. I was one of them. An alcoholic. And I belonged there with them.

I added alcoholism to the list of issues Martha was helping me with and decided to sign up for the AA 12-Step program. I saw a doctor as well who prescribed Paxil to help me manage my anger. Small steps, but critical ones.

Lessons

Martha's work with me was largely devoted to dealing with two big issues in my life that, for the first time, I realized were related: self-esteem and accountability. Neither of these are "big ticket" items for a Jehovah's Witness. The virtue of self-esteem as seen through the filter of Watchtower teachings becomes the sin of pride. And it's hard to take responsibility for your own actions when you've been raised to think that your actions are programmed by Satan, himself.

During this period, God saw fit to put me in situations that made these points in ways I shall never forget. At our first meeting, Martha introduced me to the novel idea of having

worth and knowing it. Now I found myself in a situation at
work that brought the concept into the real world.

I had changed jobs to cut down on the amount of travel I
was doing and was now working for a custom cabinetry business that created dream kitchens for high-end homes. I was
pleased to have received a promotion to management, and for
a while I was quite happy. But after a while a creeping anxiety
began to make itself known—a feeling that I was a pretender.
Not only did I not do any real work—I merely *managed* those
who did—but I couldn't *possibly* be good at managing. I had
no education to speak of. I'd barely scraped my way out of high
school, and everything I had learned since was the result of
dogged determination.

Now I became increasingly convinced that I was "faking it"
and that sooner or later my boss had to realize this. And, of
course, when he realized this, he would fire me.

Naturally the result of this line of thinking was that I
began to look for disapproval or disappointment in my boss's
every facial expression, every word, every gesture. Eventually, I
began to believe I found what I was looking for: his smiles
seemed insincere, his words ambiguous, his frowns more frequent and always directed at me. I became nervous about
meeting with him; my skin crawled when he came into my
work area.

Unable to stand it anymore, but unwilling to upset
Andrea, I called Martha and poured out my anguish on her.

She listened attentively, then said, "You finished?"

"Yes," I said, having run out of fears to shower her with.

"You're hallucinating, Dan," she told me. "Go back to
work. Concentrate on that—on what you know how to do.
This *is* a job, and you're *good* at it."

"No," I argued. "This isn't real work. I'm not doing any-thing but watching *other* people work. And Rob is bound to notice. What can I do?"

"Write it down—what you think your boss is thinking, why you think he's going to fire you, every clue that leads you to the conclusion that your days are numbered."

I did write it down, and I tried to take her advice. I really did. But it was so hard. And the next time my manager, Rob, called me into his office, I was panic-stricken.

Here it comes, I thought. *I'm going to be fired.*

I squared my shoulders and went into Rob's office to face my fate.

He rose from behind his desk, smiled, stuck out his hand, and said, "Congratulations, Dan. You've outlasted any other manager we've had in this position. You may not have a college degree, but you do great work. In fact, I wish I had more man-agers like you."

"You see?" Martha said, when I called to tell her about this miracle. "I *told* you you were hallucinating. Go back and read your notes, and the next time something like this happens, find out what's really going on. Don't act on fear. Oh, and don't call *me* until you know the *real* situation."

I went back and read my notes. They were the paranoid ramblings of a madman. Or at least they displayed an acute case of anxiety. They were, in fact, silly. I *was* good at my job. I had the knowledge and the experience and the craftsmanship to guide other people through the process of making dreams out of hardwood.

And that was lesson one: *Know your worth.* Oh, yeah—and don't confuse hallucinations with reality.

My lesson about personal responsibility and accountability

was a harder-won. There was a Mexican couple—Marguerite and Ramon—employed in the cabinetry shop. She was a team leader in assembly; he worked in the machine shop cutting wood for each order. Also in the assembly area—working under Marguerite's supervision—was Joey, a Jehovah's Witness acquaintance I'd hired.

It had not escaped my attention that Joey had little if any respect for Marguerite. He obeyed her instructions reluctantly, countered her every opinion, and generally gave her a hard time. I have no doubt it galled him to have a woman—and a Mexican woman at that—supervising his work, and his behavior bore that out.

One day as I was out in the shop, I walked into the assembly area to find Joey arguing with Marguerite over the way a cabinet door should be attached to a custom order. This was something she not only knew far better than he did, but she was his team lead; he owed her respect on both counts. Now, he loomed over this petite woman, his dialogue straying uncomfortably close to racial slurs.

The situation reminded me far too much of the way my brother Keith verbally intimidated our mom. I had defended her countless times against his aggressive behavior, one time leaping out of the pantry and clobbering him in the head with a big, heavy cookie sheet. The sudden memory chilled me and the "alpha rescuer" in me went into high gear. I stepped in and told Joey in no uncertain terms that he was putting his job in jeopardy by talking to Marguerite in this way. He owed her respect, and he'd damn well better give it to her.

He backed down and did what Marguerite had instructed him to do. And that was that, I thought. I went away feeling that I'd done a service—I'd defended the meek, rescued the damsel in distress.

Later I was out in the machine shop discussing a job with my friend and coworker, Bonita, who was half of a lesbian couple I'd hired to do sanding and antiquing. As we chatted, one of the white members of the machine shop crew unloaded on Marguerite's husband, Ramon, who was manning the radial saw.

"You stupid wetback!" the guy shouted. "You'd better hurry up with that or you're gonna put us all behind schedule! So c'mon, Chico, get a move on!"

There was no rationale for the attack; it was as if suddenly the fact that Ramon was Latino (as were Bonita and her partner Paula and half the machine crew) had suddenly pushed the guy's "bigot" button. And as near as I could tell, Ramon's speed on the saw was just fine.

Irked, I turned to Bonita and said, "That pisses me off. He's treating Ramon as if he were a damn dog!" I turned on my heel and went back to my office on the assembly floor.

That afternoon my boss, Rob, called me into his office. Adhering to Martha's advice, I read nothing into it, and went in without expectation. Imagine my shock when Rob began to counsel me about making "racist remarks."

"You can't do that here, Dan," he told me, disappointment radiating from him in waves.

"What racist remarks?" I demanded.

"Marguerite was down in the machine shop and overheard you call her husband a dog."

I was stunned. I explained what I had really said, and Rob responded with both belief and relief. But as I left his office my shock was swallowed by a growing fury at the sheer injustice of the situation. I'd *rescued* that woman, dammit! And this was the thanks I got?

By the end of the day my temper had boiled up into a murderous rage. I had a session scheduled with Martha that evening and, naturally, this episode from work was all I wanted to talk about. How could Marguerite believe I'd call her husband a dog after I'd defended her from the same sort of abuse? Did she honestly believe I'd say something like that to another Latina? She didn't know I was actually *defending* Ramon, but she would have if she'd bothered to ask Bonita what I'd said, or even confronted me about it instead of running to my boss. It just wasn't fair, and I wanted to get in Marguerite's face and tell her so. In fact, I wanted to shake her until her teeth rattled, but I was reluctant to admit that, even to Martha.

When my red rage spent itself a bit, I looked to Martha for support of my righteous indignation.

Her reaction was completely unexpected. "You're sick," she told me.

"*I'm* sick? What about *her?*"

"Dan, this woman didn't ask you to rescue her. You took it upon yourself to do that. And it's a noble thing to do, but it was a gift. You didn't have the right to give Marguerite that gift if you were going to expect something from her in return. When you perform an act of kindness, you can't do it with strings attached. You should do it because it's right, not because you're hoping for some sort of reward."

As I remember this episode, I'm struck by the fact that what Martha said is also true of my relationship with God. I had, for so long, worshipped in hope of Paradise and in fear of

Death, that the idea of doing what was right without hope of reward or fear of reprisal was alien to me.

This was lesson two: *Take responsibility for your own behavior.*

In Sickness and in Health

For a time my life was idyllic. Andrea and I were both in school, expanding our minds and our world-views. We had a lovely home, nice cars, and a new cluster of friends from the Church of Religious Science we were now attending. We were freeing ourselves from the "hooks" the Watchtower Society had sunk in our lives and our souls. I was happy, learning to control my anger and my drinking, learning to give love to family and friends…and the God I had begun to realize could be a good and kindly friend.

"If you want to see real love," I was moved to tell a coworker, "come to my house."

But when I arrived home that very evening, my house was empty. Literally. My wife and two daughters were gone, and with them, their clothing, toys, and half the furnishings.

Andrea had left me, without warning or explanation.

Oh, there was a letter on the kitchen table, but it said only, "Dan, you're a wonderful man. You're a good guy. But I've left—I've gotten off this train and I'm gone for good—never to return."

Stunned doesn't even begin to cover what I felt—or didn't feel—at this twist in the thread of my life. I went into the living room and lay on the remaining couch. I don't believe I moved for three days: I didn't eat. I didn't even really sleep. I just lay there. Until a persistent thought finally burrowed its way to the surface: *If you don't move now—get off this couch and do something—you never will. You'll die here.*

I forced myself up. I called Martha. She came over immediately. She cried with me.

And when we were both cried out, she said, "This is great, Dan. I know you don't think so now, but this is a learning experience—a time for growth. Take out your journal and write down all the ways you were a son-of-a-bitch to Andrea and your daughters while this is all still fresh in your mind. That way you'll know not to repeat the behavior."

I did that. It seemed a long list, at the top of which was my sometimes unreasonable and unmanageable anger. I was well aware of how my temper had affected my relationships with family and friends. And now I realized something else: I had intentionally kept too many things going on in my life—my job, counseling with Martha, college, Science of Mind—to fill in the gap left by my withdrawal from the Kingdom Hall...and to keep from having to look too closely at myself. In doing that, I had left too little time for Andrea and the girls, and now they were gone.

But I did it for them, I told myself. *I did all of it for them.*

I doubt that was true, but even if it was, I should have asked them if those things were what they *wanted* me to do for them. I should have communicated—made sure of the real situation—before I acted.

A little less than a week after she left, I heard from Andrea by phone. She said she was in therapy, was getting her life together.

I felt a tickle of hope—maybe then she'd come back—but she shattered that hope. She was gone for good, she assured me. Of that much she was certain.

That was not what I wanted to hear.

"Your life should be good now," she added. "You have a

good-paying job and I'm not going to ask for much for child support. So you'll have lots of money to spend on yourself. It's going to be great—you'll see."

I sincerely doubted that. "Was I a bad husband?" I asked. "Was it my anger that drove you away?"

"No," she told me. "You were a good husband. You did everything a husband could do—providing for me and the kids."

I didn't believe her. Not for a moment. But neither did I press her for what I sensed she couldn't give me—reasons, rational or otherwise. Somehow I understood what she was going through. It was her time to explore, to grow, and to find out who she was: something more than a housewife who'd married a man because her religion seemed to demand it.

I didn't try to talk her into coming back. She was a volume in my life story that I'd finished and put up on the shelf. I was too numb, at that moment, to have thoughts about my daughters. Those thoughts came later—days later, in fact. But they did come.

Who is Dan Clark?

It took several days for reality to hit me. I had to sell the house—the home that we'd been living in with our girls for seven years. It seemed too much effort to see a real estate agent or take out ads, so I simply walked down the street to the corner where our lovely new neighborhood butted up against a neighborhood that was neither so new nor so lovely.

As luck or fate or Divine Providence would have it, I saw a couple looking at a home for sale. They were in the act of taking a brochure out of the box tacked to the real estate sign when I approached them and asked, "How would you like to buy my house down the road?"

They looked across the avenue at the newer, more stately homes and said, "Oh, we couldn't possibly afford one of those."

I said, "What if I could make my house as affordable as these houses down here? What if I gave you the $25,000 equity in my house—would you buy it?"

They looked at me as if I were crazy (possibly by this time, I was) and said, "Yes."

We closed within a matter of weeks. I had cut another tie with my past and wondered how many more I'd have to cut before I was really and truly free.

Martha had lots of ideas about that. She was certain she knew why what had happened had happened and what I should do with my life from here on out. We would continue to study together on a regular basis, of course, while she showed me how to live. She knew how much I made each year and had come up with plans for how I should spend and invest it. She had done such a masterful job of investing her husband's earnings that he had been able to retire early. She had the same sort of plans for me. She also knew the perfect place for me to live.

Looking back, I feel that in many ways I needed the level of control that Martha offered. She was the spiritual analogue of a physical therapist. She took on people like me who'd been injured or disabled by the accidents of life and manhandled us, working our atrophied "muscles" until they shrieked for mercy. And my spiritual muscles were well beyond atrophy.

But I had also begun to feel that Martha needed to control the lives of others in the same way I needed to perform rescues. In fact, I suspected we were much alike in that way—both had a deep-seated need to save people. Martha once told me I used rescue to manipulate other people, to put them in debt to me.

I don't know if that was why she did it, but I saw the ultimate result of it in her husband, Gerald.

When I was first grappling with my alcoholism, Gerald was the one who came to my rescue in his own quiet way. I expressed a desire to enroll in his 12-step program and he immediately volunteered to be my sponsor. The idea imbued this quiet man with an eagerness I'd never seen in him before.

I was merely grateful for his interest and didn't think anything of it until one day I came to Martha's house for one of my sessions and found the living room empty.

"That you, Dan?" Martha's voice came from the master suite at the back of the house. "Come on in here."

I entered Martha's bedroom to find her propped up in her electronic hospital-style bed with Gerald standing to one side, head down, looking for all the world like a little boy who's just been caught with his hand in the cookie jar.

Without further ado, Martha elevated the head of her bed and said, "Gerald has something to say to you, Dan. Gerald?" She nodded to him.

"Dan," said Gerald softly, "I can't be your sponsor for AA. I'm not qualified."

"Wh-what?" I stammered. "I don't understand."

"*I'm* going to be your sponsor," said Martha. "And you're not going to do some lame-ole AA routine, either. That's just a bunch of drunks sitting around sharing their sob-stories. I'm going to design a 12-step program for you, myself."

And she did.

So now, with my life in complete disarray, Martha's nurturing began to suffocate me. I was on overload. I had to get away. I decided to move out of Loveland—after all I was commuting two hours a day to Denver to work. What could make more sense than to simply move closer to the one thing in my life that was still stable—my job?

There was an area of Denver that I drove by every day on my commute that I'd fancied living in for some time—the Tech Center area. It was a decidedly upscale urban neighborhood of town homes, lofts, and apartments surrounded by shops and restaurants. What struck me most about it was how it looked at Christmas time, aglow with warmth and light. The buildings were decorated to the nines and the trees along the boulevards looked as if stars had settled in them. It resonated with my soul.

So, I fled to Denver. Saying nothing of it to Martha, I just left, cutting off all communication with any friends I still had in Loveland. I moved into a very nice apartment in the Tech Center area when it was in full Christmas glory. My only helpers were my dear friends Bonita and Paula, but we did the move in one day. My load was light, after all; ninety percent of what remained after Andrea left I gave away to anyone who would come and haul it off.

All the things I thought were so important—the entertainment center, the full gym in the basement, all the knickknacks and things that I mistook for treasure—I gave away in exchange for my freedom. I kept only a few personal necessities—a lamp, an end table, a couch, a bed.

I loved my new place. From my front window I had a view of the Denver skyline—tall, gleaming buildings that drew the eye upward toward Heaven. It was the place I had always wanted to live...just not *alone*.

One afternoon I walked over to Target to get a few things to decorate my apartment with. When I reached the outside of the store I stood in the swirling snow, suddenly unable to remember where I was or how I had gotten there.

I recalled that I was Dan Clark. But all the things that had once defined him—his faith, his marriage, his family, his friendships, his home—all these things were gone.

Who was Dan Clark?

I wondered if I would ever know.

XIII

Learning Freedom

The Angry God

You're probably ready to hear that after I'd pulled Martha's training wheels off my life and moved to Denver I got my act together. I tried to do that. I *believed* I was doing that, but the truth was I'd spent so many years—my entire life—inside the box of Watchtower doctrine that I had no idea how to live without those constraints, without those imposed beliefs and goals.

Living a life of preparation to *leave* this world does nothing to prepare you to *exist* in it, let alone have life more abundantly, as the scriptures put it. I had never really learned how to live here, how to enjoy this life or the people who were going through it with me. That would have been counter to the teachings of my faith. And now, having squandered the love of my family, I was desperately lonely.

In an attempt to fill the spiritual void in my life, I began attending the Mile High Church of Religious Science. Martha had taken me there once the previous year when I was still thinking like a Jehovah's Witness. She wasn't trying to push me in any particular direction, she'd brought me there to hear Wayne Dyer speak since I had expressed interest in his work.

I laugh when I recall that first visit. I'd been literally afraid to touch the door handle of the church for fear God would burn my hand in anger. In spite of that, I went in and hunkered in my chair, fearing—irrationally, I know—that someone from the Kingdom Hall might find out I'd come. The lights in the huge hall dimmed, music rose, and I began to cry as I had never cried before. And I experienced something in that place that I had never experienced before—the unconditional love of God.

Hungry for that love, I began attending on a regular basis. One by one, the chronic ailments that had plagued me began to fall away. Fear of God was replaced with the possibility of loving Him as Christ said He loved me. Guilt lifted from my shoulders, and the constant pain in my stomach—caused by peptic ulcers—subsided. The ulcers themselves healed spontaneously, allowing me to be free of medication for the first time in years.

It's truly amazing what guilt and fear can do to the human body.

I had a major epiphany thanks to this church and a class called the Inner Child Journey. Yeah, I know—very New Age—but I can't deny what it did for me.

One of the exercises that I will never forget was intended to reveal what God and religion meant to each of us. It involved making a sculpture out of the people in the group to represent our childhood view of God and religion.

First you chose someone to stand in for God. I asked one of the male members of the group to go stand in the corner, fold his arms, and look angry. I positioned another two guys between me and "God," one pretending to expound from the Bible, the other pretending to expound from *The Watchtower*. Next I lined my "family" up in a row to show how they would sit during worship. So, I chose four men and a woman as stand-ins. Placing the three "boys" between "Mom and Dad," I had them face the two readers, and beyond them, the Angry God.

I looked at my human sculpture—at the religion I had illustrated—and began to cry. I sobbed for twenty minutes while my new friends comforted me.

Why, I asked myself, *is God mad at me?*

Because, my memory whispered, *after He created the Earth, Satan misled Adam and Eve and caused His plan to fail.*

God, failing? How could that happen? How had I come to believe that?

I turned my thoughts to the surrogate readers of Bible and *Watchtower*—the Elders of the Kingdom Hall. *Who are they?* I thought. *Who are they to stand between me and God?*

They were not qualified to stand in that position, to condition my faith, to tell me what to believe and not to believe. The things the "faithful and discreet slave" published were, by its own admission imperfect.

My terror of the Angry God left me in that moment of clarity. It has never returned.

The Angry Man

Now, fully out of the Kingdom Hall and on my own, starting fresh, I became deeply involved in the church. I loved it there. I felt complete—satisfied at a soul-deep level. I made new friends. For the first time in my life, I prayed to a God who I believed loved me. Who wanted the best for me. Who wanted to work through me. For the first time in my life, I was beginning to commune with God the Father in a loving way. My life began to change and I planned to become a Science of Mind practitioner.

Perhaps the changes did not come fast enough. Or perhaps I was simply not ready to take full responsibility for my own spiritual growth. Or, yet again, maybe I needed to test the love I had found—to test God. Whatever the reason, I existed in a sort of dual world, feeling spiritually complete and wonderful while I was with my friends in the church, dropping into a pit of lonely despair when I was home alone.

Some nights I came home from work furious at God. I cried out, "Why God, *why* did this happen to me? I provided for my family. I loved my children. Why did You take them from me?"

Sometimes I strove with God physically, punching futilely at the air, at the pillows on the couch, acting out Jacob's struggle with the angel at river Jabbok. I told God, "If I could only get my hands on You, I'd kill You!" After these absurd fights, I would fall into an exhausted sleep.

I began to frequent a nightclub in my neighborhood that served mostly older people—successful people, I thought. Watching them dance, talk, laugh, I felt so alone, so inadequate. They were smarter, better-educated, and had much more going on in their lives than I did. I couldn't share in their laughter; I couldn't even drink what they drank. So I sat outside their happy social circles, watching the couples, alone at my table with a bottle of water.

It was painful—like rubbing salt in an open wound—but

I did it several nights a week, telling myself I was going there for the buffet. It became a habit with me. One night I added a bit of Jack Daniels to my Coke, and soon that became a habit, too.

But I was a responsible drinker; whenever the alcohol began to interfere with me paying my bills on time or feeling good about my progress, I would cut back on my visits to the club and pull myself together. But that, too, caused me pain. If I didn't go out, how was I ever to meet the woman who could become my new partner in life?

Limbo

Desperate people do desperate things, often without realizing how dangerous those things are. My desperation kept me going to the club, kept me drinking, made me less and less attentive to the job that had served as my point of stability during this topsy-turvy period of my life.

I thought things were looking up when I made some new friends at the club and began to do more than watch other people having fun. These new friends seemed like decent folks—folks I could trust. One of them, an older gentleman named Shaun, needed a place to stay temporarily. I offered my apartment. He was a good roommate, neat, orderly—as I said, a gentleman.

"You know," he told me one evening when I was apparently radiating neediness, "we don't have to be alone. We can have a couple of girls come over for about fifty dollars or so."

I had no idea what he meant. He showed me. The next thing I knew a couple of women arrived to perform sex. At the time I thanked God, as if He had delivered them to my door Himself. I was so hungry for a woman's touch that, prostitutes or not, they seemed like angels to me. In fact, I didn't think of it as prostitution at the time. I only knew that I felt so much better just to be held, just to be intimate with someone. It was expensive, but it was worth it. It became habit with me too, whenever I could afford it.

Then one night at the club, a miracle occurred. At least it looked like a miracle from where I stood. I was on the dance floor when this beautiful, well-dressed young woman walked up, introduced herself as Shelley, and started dancing with me. At the end of the evening she asked for my phone number and said, "I'll call you."

To my surprise, she did. She invited me to her house and I went. I don't know what I expected. It wasn't what I found: a gang-infested neighborhood where every household hid behind wrought iron bars from the callused, hardened people who roamed the streets. I almost drove away, but my desperate desire for a relationship spurred me on.

Shelley met me at the door wearing a silk robe. She led me to the bedroom, but on the way there we passed the living room where I saw her two little boys watching TV. Again, I almost bolted. This felt so wrong.

Shelley very soon made it feel right. So right, I stayed with her and her kids for the better part of two months, frequently missing work.

I wanted to make things right for Shelley and her boys, too, so I leveraged my high-paying job and my excellent credit to buy a house for the four of us. Shelley reacted strangely to this. She didn't need a big house, she said. The whole idea seemed to make her nervous. I pushed forward anyway, closing the deal as quickly as possible.

The day we moved in, I lost my job. No wonder, considering how badly I'd been neglecting it. I suddenly realized why Shelley was so tense about the move. Her rent-controlled apartment cost her $80 per month—but with a three year waiting list, there was no going back. I hadn't given her security; I'd taken away the only security she and her children had.

In short order, I'd chased the promise of a $65,000 per year job across the country to Virginia, dragging Shelley and her family with me. The job was a scam. Not only did I not get the promised sign-on bonus, but my first paycheck bounced. The out-of-state business owners swore they would make it good, but I had a motto: One bounce and you're out.

We managed to sell enough household goods to move back to our abandoned home in Colorado, but there was no work there for either of us—my field was highly specialized, and I'd thoroughly burned my bridges.

That was when Shelley leveled with me about her past and her felony conviction for prostitution. She had, for many years, made her living just like the women Shaun had called to my apartment. They had seemed a piece of Heaven, but the thought of Shelley doing that was sheer Hell. Now she suggested that her sexual talents could get us out of debt and back on our feet in no time. I rejected the idea.

At what surely had to be the lowest point, Shelley disappeared for three days. Recovering her led me to discover that she was a crack addict. Back home, she once again offered to use her body to bail us out. Again I said "no." We tried to find jobs doing anything else—cleaning houses, flipping burgers, anything. Shelley even begged illegal immigrants for leads. We maxed out our last credit card, wrote our last bad check.

And I drove Shelley to her first appointment as a call girl.

It was like a cosmic game of Limbo—how low can you go?

I bottomed out as I lay on the bed in the house from which we were about to be evicted—flies everywhere, no water, no electricity—and reviewed all the men I'd delivered Shelley to in the last several weeks. Old men, young men, rich men, poor men—all sexually addicted.

I got up and left everything behind again—the house, Shelley, her kids, all of it—and begged a former employer for a job. It was another trap. I was underpaid to the point that I couldn't even afford a place to stay and was reduced to sleeping on a thin mattress on the floor of my boss's fifth bedroom. I was behind in my child support and had started bankruptcy proceedings. I had no prospects, no friends, no way out.

So I made one.

I took a chance and called a guy named Dylan who owned a shop in Castle Rock. He took me on, offering me a "good faith" advance of $1000. He offered me $50,000 per year, co-signed on an apartment and a car, and told other people of my dire situation. His friends even came to my rescue, giving me everything I needed to furnish an apartment.

A turnabout? Yes, in more ways than one. I had been the career rescuer of "poor souls." Now other people—people I hardly knew—were returning the favor. I soon had a job, a place to live, and friends…but there was still one thing missing. I was still alone in life.

In this state of abject isolation, I turned to God and said, "Lord, somewhere out there is a woman. I don't know where she is, but You do. I don't know what's good for me or bad, but You do. I surrender. You lead me to her. You show me where she is."

Oddly, the sense of desperation left me after that. I knew that some day she would simply show up. And I'd know her when I saw her.

XIV

Angels

Steve

About this same time I realized that prayer was really beginning to work in my life. "Let go and let God" is a cliché, but it's a good cliché. I began to take stock of where I was and where I was going—and where I *wanted* to go. Part of this assessment was the realization that I wanted to find a way to make enough money to minimize the struggle for material things in my life. I more or less asked God to send me a mentor. He did.

The answer to this prayer arrived in the form of Steve, a happy-go-lucky fellow who informed me that he was a millionaire. "Right now, I don't have two nickels to rub together, but when a couple of my deals come through, I'll have a fortune."

Yeah, right, I thought. "What do you do, exactly?" I asked aloud.

"I'm in International Mergers and Acquisitions. Simply put, I make deals for people."

"That's your job? You make deals?"

He laughed. "I haven't had a j-o-b for thirty-five years and I don't plan on ever having one."

"J-o-b?" I repeated.

"Just Over Broke. You know, one of those deals where you don't think for yourself or use your native talent. Where you pursue someone else's idea of a calling until all the creativity is sucked out of you."

"Then how do you make a living," I asked him, "if you don't have a job?"

"You don't need a *job*," Steve told me. "You just need to find a way to make money. Do that, and you're free."

I must have seemed skeptical because, as we lunched together, he showed me the contracts he was working on. Signed and dated contracts. Company logos I recognized. And they weren't million dollar contracts, they were *multi*-million dollar contracts.

"Can you teach me how to do this?" I asked. "Can you teach me how to be independent?"

"Sure," he said. "But remember, I'm not rolling in money yet. Wait until these contracts close. Then see what you think."

Later he made a passing reference to the fact that he wasn't very happy with the temporary living situation he had, and I invited him to come stay with me. Yes, I suspect most of you are rolling your eyes and thinking, "What a rube." You're thinking Steve was probably a con man. You're thinking, "If something sounds too good to be true, it probably is." But read on.

As Steve taught me about the way finance and capitalism

worked, I became aware that the two things I wanted and needed were to be financially independent and to have a good wife. He was taking care of the finance part, I figured, so I suggested we go out "clubbing" some evenings so I could work on the other half of the goal.

"There's nothing good to be found in a dive, Dan," he told me. "Not for a good man like you. You're a better person than you give yourself credit for."

"But I've made so many mistakes," I protested.

"Yes, but you *know* they were mistakes. Bad people, stupid people, don't know when they've made mistakes. They just keep making them. You're a lot smarter than a lot of the MBAs I've dealt with in financial institutions."

I didn't know whether he was flattering me, or if he was telling the truth. I decided to take it as truth. As Jesus comments in the book of Matthew (7), *"Ask, and it will be given to you; seek, and you will find; knock, and it will be opened to you. For everyone who asks receives, and he who seeks finds, and to him who knocks it will be opened. Or what man is there among you who, if his son asks for bread, will give him a stone? Or if he asks for a fish, will he give him a serpent? If you then, being evil, know how to give good gifts to your children, how much more will your Father who is in heaven give good things to those who ask Him!"* (New King James Version)

I had asked for a mentor—or perhaps for an angel. I had reason to hope I'd found one, and even more so after I'd dragged poor Steve to the clubs with me a few times in spite of his protests. After a few visits, it became obvious to him that I had a drinking problem. Eventually he refused to go to the clubs with me, but he would always be there at closing to pick me up so I wouldn't kill myself trying to get home.

"You're never going to get ahead drinking like that," he told me. "And you need to at least get to more upscale places."

Against all fear of not being educated or good enough for the places Steve suggested, I let him take me to some of the most elegant clubs I have ever seen in my life. Valet parking, for the nice, new, high-end cars, men in Armani suits, women in diamonds and Gucci shoes.

I stood on the sidewalk and told him I couldn't go in. I felt as if I was wearing the social equivalent of a *Kick me* sign on my butt.

Steve simply couldn't understand what was going on in my head. "Christ, Dan. I don't know how such an intelligent, good-looking guy can be so intimidated by people like them."

I didn't know either.

He prevailed that evening and dragged me into the club. Within a short time, I was dancing with a woman who appeared to be quite well-to-do and chatting with men and women of the same ilk who seemed to like me. I couldn't believe that this was *me*, Dan Clark, perennial loser.

These outings became habitual—we'd go from one fancy place to another, each more exclusive than the next. I think Steve intentionally put me in positions that forced me to face my fears and feelings of inadequacy and overcome them. He also began to show increasing impatience with my work situation.

"You work twelve hour days and make only $180 a day," he observed. "That's not right, Dan. You're making $800 less than you should be. You're worth $1,000 a day."

At first I took that as encouragement, but after six months without any of his deals closing, his manifest disappointment in me was beginning to cloy. Who was he to tell me how much money I should be making? He wasn't making any at all and living out of a single suitcase.

Then one day he asked me, "How would you like to be in a promotional movie?" And before I could think about it I said, "yes."

"Good. We're shooting Thursday morning."

Thursday morning I was getting ready for work when Steve popped his head into my room and said, "Remember, you're not going into work today—you're going with me. We're making a movie!"

Fear rose up inside me. I couldn't afford to miss a day of work and said as much.

Steve stood in the door and glared at me. "You promised! This is more important than your job, dammit. You're not going in today. So call that jerk boss of yours and tell him...whatever."

So, I called in sick, put on my suit, and went to the "shoot." The place Steve took me really was a movie production set. I was asked to play a lawyer. It was incredible: being in the streets of downtown Denver with real camera crews; smelling fresh, clean air instead of lacquer; mingling with people in clean clothes instead of stain-encrusted overalls.

We completed the movie that afternoon. On the way home I told Steve, "I'm never going to work for anybody— ever again!"

"Like I said," Steve reminded me, "you don't need a j-o-b, you just need to learn how to make money."

I started an LLC Corporation, opened a bank account in the name of my new business, and I began making phone calls to get things rolling. But Steve had other ideas—or at least he had an idea for how I could make money while I waited for my "ship" to come in.

"Have you thought about selling cars?" he asked. His son was a top salesman, it seemed, and had once made over $10,000 in a single month. Steve was sure I could do the same if not better.

I was terrified. I applied to a dealership, interviewed, and waited patiently for a week, mentally chanting my new mantra: $10,000 per month, clean clothes, no more *eau de lacquer*.

I got the job and went into intensive training so as to best serve the elite customers who frequented this dealership. I aced the Internet training, then moved on to the "live" instruction. The prospect of learning something new was exhilarating.

But I was still empty. Alone. Having a roommate was great, and I valued Steve's friendship immensely, but I wanted a relationship with a woman. I wanted a wife—someone to grow with spiritually,,someone with substance and integrity.

So, one night as I lay in bed shedding lonely tears, I recommitted myself to surrender. "Father, I know You, I trust in You, I surrender to You." I just let that prayer go—and fell asleep feeling assured.

Angela

The next day I went to offsite training and testing for dealership sales reps. I was sitting in the training room when a lovely, blonde woman sat down next to me. Although she was beautiful, there was something fragile about her. Perhaps it was a certain vulnerability that showed in her sweet expression or a wariness about her eyes. Something in the way she wore her clothing, the way she sat, the way she moved, gave me the eerie feeling that something terrible and traumatic had happened to this woman.

During a lull in our schedule, I walked into the break room to find her talking on the phone—something about real estate. She was very deep into her conversation, but still took the time to look up and say "Hi" with a big smile that touched my heart.

I sat at a table and sipped a cup of coffee. When she hung up, I offered her coffee and a donut from the copious supply they always have at these training sessions to keep the trainees buzzing.

We exchanged names—hers was Angela.

I don't know how it came up, exactly, maybe I asked her or maybe she felt the same thing about me that I had about her. Whatever started it, she briefly shared with me the trauma she was just beginning to recover from. She'd been in a quasi-Christian cult, she told me,, along with her sisters, her husband, her children, and her nephew. She had recently discovered her husband's infidelity and, even more recently, had escaped him and the cult. She was desperate to cut the ties. But, she added, her escape had come at a terrible price. Her family had rejected her; her children wouldn't even speak to her.

How well I understood—understood the confusion, the chaos, the rejection that she was going through. My heart went out to this courageous woman and, impulsively, I put my arms around her and hugged her.

We sat side-by-side throughout the rest of the training. On the last day we had lunch together on the lawn of the training facility. We began discussing scripture and talking about our difficult spiritual paths. I knew she was a good woman, a spiritual woman. She literally glowed as we talked.

"Do you know you're shining right now?" I asked her, and she laughed. Later in the conversation I asked, "Do you ever feel like nobody understands you but God? That you're all alone in the world?"

"Yes, actually I do," she told me.

We bonded at that moment and began a true friendship. I was not to be her rescuer, nor she mine. We were equals, each striving to raise a new life out of the ashes of the old.

With our training over, I didn't hear from Angela again for about a month. We both began selling cars and doing quite well although it wasn't $10,000 a month. In fact, although I learned quickly, it seemed as if I still didn't have enough money between child support, car payments, rent, and utilities—I was living responsibly now and it showed in my bank balance.

I started to think maybe I could do occasional furniture touch-up work. Maybe through some miracle of God, and with Steve's constant encouragement, I could get my business going. And it would take a miracle; all of the "feelers" I'd put out returned no evidence that there was any work out there.

Steve said philosophically, "Don't worry. The money will come. You're on a tightrope, buddy. All you gotta do is not look down. Have a little faith."

He repeated this over and over, all the while telling me that if I stayed with the car dealership, I could make that $10,000 per month. But I decided after a couple of months selling cars that it wasn't for me. It wasn't that I wasn't *good* at it—I was. Very. But it didn't engage me. It wasn't my calling. I wasn't interested in cars.

But I *could* sell things. What if, I thought, I could sell my woodworking skills? I was already a master of that craft. I just had to convince other people that I was.

Angela encouraged me. In fact, she did more than encourage me. She typed my correspondence, sent hundreds of emails, made phone calls, set up my books, worked on my website, got someone to create a promotional video, and made flyers for the new business. She even loaned me money for business supplies out of what she made holding down two or three jobs.

She believed in me more than I did in myself.

The day I found an eviction notice on my front door and realized I was about $3,000 behind in my bills, and that my ex-wife was going to call me every day until I caught up on child support, Steve still insisted that the money would come.

I went for a walk on the trail behind the apartment building and addressed God, saying, "I should go back and get a real job. I'm nobody. I don't have the skills it takes to run a business and I'm working so hard I don't even have time to find customers."

God was silent.

"The evidence is clear," I argued, "the eviction notice on my door, Andrea's phone calls, my bank balance."

God was still silent.

I stopped and looked up at the sky. "I *can't* go back to work. I've already worked for everyone along the front range, burned my bridges, worn myself out. I can't *do* it anymore!"

God seemed to turn a deaf ear to my outburst.

When I returned to the apartment, Steve was waiting for me with a big smile and a surprise guest—a business associate of his named Lisa.

Lisa shook my hand and said, "Thanks for helping my partner out, Dan. I owe you something for that." She handed me a check for $4,000.

I couldn't believe my eyes. Steve was right: You didn't need a job. You just needed to find a way to make money.

Lisa's check paid all my back bills. She also paid the rent on Steve's behalf for the next three months. And, as I continued to make my hopeful phone calls, searching out customers, the tide came in. I was caught in a wave of work such as I'd never seen before—job after job after job rolled up onto the shores of my new business. The money was incredible—$1,500 for this job, $2,500 for the next, $5,000 for the next.

Suddenly I was making more money in a day than I had in a week working for someone else. I was making about $1,000 a day, and not reporting to anybody—not doing someone else's bidding. It was a strange feeling. Suddenly I was a business owner. Sure, I now had a whole raft of new things to learn: bookkeeping, organization, scheduling. And I had taxes to pay and materials to buy. But I was independent of all but God.

In the midst of this, I got a call from Angela. It was growing increasingly difficult for her to stay at her mother's, she told me, to be in a home that was divided along lines of faith.

"I need to get out of here, Dan, so I can sort things out and heal. What can I do?"

I suggested that she move into my apartment complex. The places were inexpensive because they were outside city limits, and it was beautiful, to boot.

She hesitated, but I assured her that she could make it and that I would help. She could work for me from time to time doing touch-up and repairs if she needed money above her car sales job to make ends meet. Just four months after leaving the cult and her husband, she moved into the apartment complex and we began dating.

Steve, of course, knew where this was headed. I was falling

in love. It was clear to both of us that we were going to have to part company. I felt badly about this; Steve had done so much for me, and his "deals" still hadn't come through.

"I'll be fine," he assured me. "Everything I need fits into one bag."

About three months later, he moved out with no hard feelings. To my knowledge, Steve's "ship" never came in. But mine finally had.

After dating for only a short time, I knew I wanted to marry Angela. But she felt strongly that she needed time to heal, to be sure of herself. She wanted to come to me whole. She was so certain that this was God's will for her and for us that I grudgingly agreed that we would wait one year to talk seriously of marriage. I sensed she was right, but I was nervous that I might lose her if we waited that long.

She was right, of course. Both of us had so much baggage from our previous relationships and religious entanglements that we were in no condition to even be certain of our own selves, let alone each other. That year allowed us time to heal our wounds, to rebuild our dignity, to replenish our souls, to get our heads clear.

We were married in August of 2005, very much in love.

XV

The Book of Me

*Note: Scriptural quotes in this chapter are
from the New King James Bible.*

Programmed

Looking at it with 20/20 hindsight, I see that I was programmed to have a narrow world view. The Watchtower Society created absolute polarities of right and wrong, virtue and sin, us and them. It said, along with many other religious sects today, "We have God. He belongs to us. If you want God, just do as we say." Deceptively simple.

Any faith has a responsibility to ask its followers to try to live up to the standards laid down in its scriptures and to protect them from spiritual harm. But when an organization speaks as if for God and fixes absolute doctrines, when it punishes the breakage of those doctrines with complete removal from the congregation—essentially announcing that this person no longer belongs to God—that organization bears a *huge* responsibility to be certain those doctrines come from God.

Yet, in the case of the Watchtower Society, while the statements of doctrine are absolute and given in the voice of authority, *the organization itself claims no such authority.*

Take blood transfusions as an example. For many years the doctrine on transfusion was: "Whether whole or fractional, one's own or someone else's, transfused or injected, it is wrong." This pronouncement allows no argument. So it's no surprise that in answer to the question of whether transfusion was grounds for disfellowshipping, the WTS said, "The inspired Holy Scriptures say 'yes.'"

When it comes to the End of Times prophecy, the literature is equally certain. "Today, a small percentage of mankind can still recall the dramatic events of 1914," said the *Watchtower* in 1992, then asked, "Will that elderly generation pass away before God saves the earth from ruin? Not according to Bible prophecy."

Both passages show that the WTS not only spoke with assumed authority, but justified it on the basis of being authorized to interpret the Holy Scriptures. This was also true of doctrines relating to whether a woman could claim to have been raped, whether or not we should celebrate Christ's birth or our own, even who could really be considered a Christian.

It should be obvious how far-reaching the effects of these teachings are: Married couples have put off having children in fear of Armageddon. Young people have refused to be "brainwashed" by "student counselors who encourage one to pursue higher education." Working men and women have failed to provide for their retirement because they believed they would not have to worry about it with the End so near. Worse, families have been split, people have died, believers have been humiliated and driven from their communities.

My own family, for example, is thoroughly fractured. Because of the absoluteness of Watchtower theology, my mother—who is still in and out of institutions—does not speak to me. My brothers, likewise, shun me. I have no friends left from that part of my life. To associate with me is to invite disfellowshipping.

The most stunning idea of all, to me, is this: *that at one moment one of these doctrines is an unbreakable, spiritual law for which you can lose your eternal salvation and the next it is a matter of individual conscience.*

No, I take it back—that's *not* the most stunning idea. It is this: that rather than taking responsibility for the consequences of their authoritative pronouncements, the Watchtower Society first blamed the believers themselves ("...some...have planned their lives according to a mistaken view..."), *then* claimed that its writings were "never inspired, never perfect."

I would argue that you can't have it both ways: you cannot be at once absolute *and* imperfect, authoritative *and* fallible, right *and* wrong.

This raises tremendous questions: If the WTS has been fallible in its pronouncements about such things as the end of the world or blood transfusions, then how can one believe that any of its other pronouncements are any more absolute? If the leadership of the Watchtower Society is neither perfect nor inspired, how can they claim the authority to set doctrine about how believers should live their lives?

For me the answers are clear: One *cannot* believe in the absolute nature of these doctrines, nor can the Watchtower Society claim any authority to set those doctrines in the first place. I am reminded of Jesus' words in Matthew 15:7-9:

Well did Isaiah prophesy about you, saying: 'These people draw near to Me with their mouth, and honor Me with their lips, but their heart is far from Me. And in vain they worship Me, teaching as doctrines the commandments of men.'

Life in Abundance

In the Book of John 10:10 Christ says, *I have come that they might have life and might have it in abundance.* After over forty years in the Kingdom Hall, I had to *leave* to find that life. Why? Because the concept of life within the Watchtower Society is based on short-term thinking. The world is always mere moments away from destruction, therefore having any kind of life in this world outside the Kingdom Hall is not only wrong, but impossible. This forces the believer to put the emphasis on doing in this life only what he thinks will help him in the life soon to come, whether that life is in an earthly Paradise or in Heaven.

Jesus, Himself, did not ask us to focus on this. He placed His emphasis somewhere else entirely:

The first of all the commandments is: 'Hear, O Israel, the Lord our God, the Lord is one. And you shall love the Lord your God with all your heart, with all your soul, with all your mind, and with all your strength.' This is the first commandment. And the second, like it, is this: 'You shall love your neighbor as yourself.' There is no other commandment greater than these.
—Mark 12:29, 30

There is nothing in this "first of all commandments" about any of the myriad doctrines that make up the articles of faith of many churches. Those doctrines tend to dwell on things like our understanding of the exact nature of God, of Christ's divinity and humanity, of the meaning of the crucifixion, of the nature of the "spiritual body" that is resurrected, etc. This commandment is about love alone. Love for God, love for our fellow human beings. Jesus repeats this commandment to love in various ways throughout the Gospels. It is the last commandment He gives His disciples before His arrest in Gethsemane, which surely shows how important it is.

Many fundamentalist doctrines today revolve around the same beliefs that I grew up with: the world's destruction is at hand, so focus all your energy on getting to heaven. These beliefs can be so time- and energy-consuming that the believer has little energy for love and little time in which to *show* that love.

Relieved of the expectation that the world would end at any moment, I came to a crushing realization: I was prepared to die for God, but I had no idea how to *live* for Him.

It's quite common for people coming out of religious experiences like mine to turn, not to another form of faith, but to *no* faith at all. Having been disappointed by one religion they throw away *all* religion. I think there are a number of reasons for this. One is that having been damaged by something wearing the guise of God, they are afraid of being damaged further by yet another false religious experience. And so, when many of these people at last escape the box in which they've been imprisoned, they blame God for the existence of the box. They react with fear and anger: fear of change, of being "wrong," of punishment at the hand of God—anger at having been deceived.

It's a form of grieving, really: *they have just died to all of their old belief systems.*

But I'd come to the conclusion that I could no longer blame God for *my* imprisonment. He didn't create the box I was born into. I saw this most clearly during my Inner Child Journey experience at Mile High. I saw that people (Elders, the leaders of the WTS, fellow believers, etc.) had interposed themselves between me and God, had filtered His communication with me, and obscured my vision of Him. *They* can be blamed for putting themselves in that position, and *I* can be blamed for allowing them to do it for so long, but blaming God makes no sense to me at all.

Change is scary. It's hard. If you believe it's impossible to trust your ability to tell truth from falsehood, it's even scarier. That was why I stayed so long in my own box, why I lived in quiet discontent and desperation when at any time I could have stepped through the steel door and learned who I was, *why* I was, and what I could give to the world. Fear trapped me. Guilt accused me of deserving my entrapment.

Wayne W. Dyer tells a story of water bugs who live in the safe, warm, comfortable depths of a pond. On occasion one of the water bugs swims to the surface never to return. The other water bugs are afraid to follow, and so they don't see that the bugs who swim to the surface are transformed into something new: a creature with the capacity for flight, a creature who now experiences the freedom of the air, the brightness of sunlight. These flying creatures cannot go back to their old lives in the pond, and the water bugs cannot conceive of the new life outside the pond. Communication is impossible; these two creatures can no longer relate to each other.

The moral of the tale is simple: Our view of our physical world is limited by our life experience, so is our view of the vast spiritual world.

We're like books that begin filling up with writing on the day of our birth—entries are made by our parents, our siblings, our schools, our spiritual leaders, ourselves. We are each the *Book of Me* and we are convinced that the words in our book are true.

I would like to challenge the reader to consider the idea that perhaps our pages are crammed so full of the scribblings of ourselves and others that we have left no room for God to write upon them. Perhaps we need to tear some of the old pages out and say, "All right, Father, here's the pen, *You* write the story."

Final Thoughts from
a Prodigal Son

The Still, Small Voice

My life now is solid, harmonious, and synchronistic. Angela and I are blessed. Our love has continued to grow, our business to flourish beyond our wildest dreams. It doesn't hurt that ours is a match made in heaven in any number of levels from the spiritual to the material. I am a master craftsman and Angela is an excellent executive secretary. Together, we have achieved both love and independence—two ingredients that have gone into the writing of this book. The other ingredient is faith. I can say truthfully that I have never seen anyone in my entire life demonstrate such faith as Angela. Faith in me, faith in God, faith in us.

But beyond having a beautiful wife, a wonderful career,

and a successful business, I have a relationship with my Divine Father that resonates with me at a soul level. I take deep satisfaction in my walk with God. My road may not be anyone else's, but it's right for me.

I have learned a great deal from my experiences, as dire as some of them were. I have learned that God is everywhere present for all of us, and that if we only listen, we will hear His voice within ourselves, see His face in the faces of others. I have learned that we can become whole; we can become sound in mind; we can become grounded; we can become the miracle God meant us to be simply because we are made in *His* likeness and image. I have come to understand that there is a great need for us to know the truth for ourselves, to become authentic individuals.

There comes a time, I believe, that each of us will hear God's Voice and be called to follow it to find Him for ourselves. In some cases, such as my own, this leads to a monumental, life-ravaging decision. For me the need to make that decision was a sort of friction, a divine discontent. I experienced discomfort, frustration, fear, anger, guilt, and despair as I was faced with situations that my belief system had not prepared me for.

I now believe this friction was a whisper from the Creator calling me to find my path to Him—to find my true Self. Proverbs 3:5-6 says: "Trust in the Lord with all your heart, and lean not on your own understanding; In all your ways acknowledge Him, and He shall direct your paths."

Will we let God's Holy Spirit, God's invisible presence, guide our lives or will we continue to walk a maze of dysfunctional paths, experiencing life that is less than abundant? Can we pause for a moment to say, "what if?" Can we surrender to

God at depth? Can we love ourselves enough to face disapproval, disappointment, and anger from close friends and relatives in order to become our true selves? Can we acknowledge and face our fear of being wrong, of being alone, and move forward anyway?

Can we come to the realization that we are not what other people have programmed us to be?

This is The Great Question that we are trying to answer: How do we short-circuit our programming? How do we get out of our boxes? Whether we are Jews or Muslims, Jehovah's Witnesses or Pentecostals, atheists or agnostics, how do we break the surface of the pond and take to the air? And believe me when I say that no matter how dark our lives seem to be, how much our bodies weigh us down, or how uneducated our minds are, we *can* experience flight!

One way to stay out of the box—to keep from being trapped in the conceptions of other people—is not to enter the box in the first place. This is hard, of course, especially if you're born into a particular culture or philosophy. But I think we gain the ability to at least open the box (the mind) the moment we *realize* that it is only a recording and playback device, and that we are much, much more than the sum of our recorded experiences.

We are made-up people…in any number of ways. We are made up of our accumulated knowledge and experiences, both material and emotional. The face we show to ourselves and our fellow human beings is made up by our experiences and by the people in our lives. Our minds are made up, too, by those same forces, and often we don't even recognize it.

A commonly used metaphor says that life is a journey, and each of us is on a road. We buzz down our road, crossing those driven by other people, often unaware that there are literally millions of streets, avenues, broad boulevards, vast freeways, and quiet or mysterious country lanes we could be traveling. We get highway hypnosis—we are mesmerized by life, convinced of the ultimate reality of *our* reality. We grow inured to pain and discontent and accustomed to mediocrity. We are comfortable with the ruts in our road, no matter how rough a ride they give us.

Driving our road, we each develop a mental map of the way things are, and we are reluctant to change course. We are on autopilot.

Take me, for example—I'd been on autopilot since childhood. But if we only lift our heads to see the whole map—what a difference that can make! One or two degrees on a compass, that's all it takes, and we find ourselves in a whole new country!

We must each make that decision, take that step of faith, that turn in the road. My life changed when I did it. When I put my life in God's hands and didn't try to control everything, when I gave up needing to be right and have all the answers, when I learned to be content with the mystery of the moment and not worry so much about my roadmap, life worked amazingly well. With that single act of faith, God met me more than halfway.

We can all learn to do that, to demonstrate our faith by being content in not knowing when the world will end, or exactly how much faith is enough, or what exact form we will take after death. We can demonstrate our faith by truly loving each other. In fact, Christ tells us that if we are to stay connected to *His* love we *must* do this.

What Works for Me

I've done a lot of thinking about the road I took out of my particular box or boxes. I would like to encourage the reader to think about creating his or her own roadmap, finding the compass to set out on an individual journey of discovery.

I can't tell you how to do it. For one thing, each one of us is different, and our roads are different as well, though the goal—finding our true selves, learning to love and be loved, connecting with the ultimate Reality—is the same.

There are a number of things I've found critical to progress in my spiritual journey. I share them in the hope that they will spur reflection and action.

Things I learned:

- To trust in the Lord with all my heart and let Him direct my path. (Proverbs 3:5,6)
- To live by the Greatest Commandment (Mark 12:29, 30—called the *Shema Israel* by those of the Jewish faith): *"...love the Lord your God with all your heart, with all your soul, with all your mind, and with all your strength....love your neighbor as yourself."*
- To love myself. The *Shema Israel* suggested to me that I couldn't love my neighbor until I learned to love myself. Loving myself and loving others went hand in hand. The more I loved God (who is the source of love), and the more I loved myself, the more natural it became for me to love others.
- To pray regularly and, while in prayer, to be myself. To pour my heart out to God. To be honest with Him...and with myself.
- To commune with God and with my own spirit regularly. In addition to praying—which is *talking* to God—I learned to commune with God in silence, and really *listen* for Him. To let Him work on my heart and

soul to heal, teach, and give me an understanding heart and a perceptive mind. *"But seek first the kingdom of God and His righteousness,"* says Christ, *"and all these things shall be added to you."* If God promises to bless us if we ask for bread (Matthew 7:7-12) how much more will He bless us if we ask for *Him?*

- To be totally committed to God at all costs and *act* as if my prayers had already been answered. When I was trying to accomplish the goal of starting up my own business, I didn't just beg God to make it happen. I took every step I could on my own to build a mechanism by which God could answer that prayer. It's a covenant of sorts: if I do my part, God will do His.

Amen

I once called myself a Jehovah's Witness through and through. I was wrong. I was *never* a Jehovah's Witness. I was always and simply a child of God. When I put aside the colorful little Watchtower guides and read the scriptures on my own, when I remove the intermediaries between me and God, I see that His message as delivered through Christ is not about blood transfusions or voting, celebrating holidays or birthdays, or preparing for the end of the world by withdrawing from it.

It is about love.

This love is what enables me to have more abundant life, to know my own worth, to accept responsibility for my own spiritual growth. As I grow, I learn even more about how to love, not just my wife and children and my extended and spiritual families, but my fellow human beings *everywhere*.

So, I go forward into life not so much preaching or teaching, but *being*. Being the love, being the joy, being the peace right now, in this moment and forever. After all, if God, Himself, can shower His blessings on any who ask, seek, or knock at His door, how can we *not* do likewise?

* * *

"Though I speak with the tongues of men and of angels, but have not love, I have become sounding brass or a clanging cymbal. And though I have the gift of prophecy, and understand all mysteries and all knowledge, and though I have all faith, so that I could remove mountains, but have not love, I am nothing. And though I bestow all my goods to feed the poor, and though I give my body to be burned, but have not love, it profits me nothing.

Love suffers long and is kind; love does not envy; love does not parade itself, is not puffed up; does not behave rudely, does not seek its own, is not provoked, thinks no evil; does not rejoice in iniquity, but rejoices in the truth; bears all things, believes all things, hopes all things, endures all things.

Love never fails. But whether there are prophecies, they will fail; whether there are tongues, they will cease; whether there is knowledge, it will vanish away. For we know in part and we prophesy in part. But when that which is perfect has come, then that which is in part will be done away.

When I was a child, I spoke as a child, I understood as a child, I thought as a child; but when I became a man, I put away childish things. For now we see in a mirror, dimly, but then face to face. Now I know in part, but then I shall know just as I also am known. And now abide faith, hope, love, these three; but the greatest of these is love."

—The Apostle Peter, 1 Corinthians 13: 1-13

Afterword

About This Book

When Angela and I were dating, I told her that I wanted to write this book. I wanted to tell my story in an effort to help others find their way to a healthier, happier life. If I could do it, I told her, if I could fight my way out of a box, so could others. I wanted to offer those others hope.

Angela took me seriously. She got on the Internet and starting looking for ghostwriters. That's how she found Arbor Books. She immediately sent off an email to Arbor explaining that we were looking for someone to write my story.

Arbor co-founder Larry Leichman called us personally to tell us that he was excited about the book and would like to see it written. He took a lot of time to carefully explain what we could do to get started—chiefly, to start coming up with elements for a story line. We did that, but there were a couple of obstacles to our efforts. I was reluctant to relive some of the events in my life. They'd hurt plenty the first time—I wasn't that keen on going through them again. But I was beginning to realize I'd have to if my words of encouragement were to be meaningful. The second obstacle was absurdly mundane: we didn't know where we were going to come up with the money to pay a ghostwriter.

After talking to the folks at Arbor on and off for about a year and agonizing over the finances, I decided to try to write the book on my own. We hired a writing coach who met with me via telephone and coached me on how to write my story. She had me write about different events in my life, then encouraged me to use my imagination to expand on these to bring in more emotional content and detail. It was painful, grueling, and even rewarding in some ways, but I didn't get much useful material for a book.

It took us a while to realize that we weren't getting our money's worth from this arrangement and that often what I produced wasn't *real*—it was just me imagining what *might* be, when what had *really* happened was emotional enough. We turned to Arbor again and verbally agreed that we'd hire one of their ghostwriters to tell the story.

It looked like we were back on track until we got a call from a friend of mine who invited us to come hear this "wonderful guy" speak at a free seminar on personal healing. We went to hear Mr. Wonderful that same night, and he *was* wonderful. Plus, he had a program that was guaranteed to heal our lives forever.

It sounded great—so great that we visited his home office for a face-to-face meeting. At this meeting he evaluated the answers we'd given to a bunch of survey questions and "interviewed" us to judge if we were sincere about wanting to change our lives. Only if we were sincere would he offer us a spot in his program.

And it would only cost about $1200.

Yes, I hear you: *Here goes Dan again. When will he learn that if it sounds too good to be true...?*

Apparently I had not yet learned this. I had Angela write a check to Mr. Wonderful to reserve our spot in his seminar. And I had her call Arbor to explain that we were going to postpone writing the book. Yes, we realized we'd already agreed to do this with them and sent a check. But we felt that we simply *must* go through this incredible program that guaranteed to transform our lives and heal all of our past injuries—emotional, mental, and spiritual. We'd most certainly come out whole, functioning human beings, which would enable us to write a better book.

That was when Larry called us again, afraid we were about to be ripped off by a spiritual scam artist. He begged us to be careful and wary of anyone who guaranteed that we'd be made whole just by taking a course.

"It took years to get to where you are right now," Larry told us. "And this guy is promising you the moon. For one thing, nobody is ever completely whole, and for another, you want to write from your pain, because that is the most powerful writing there is."

"But we need to *heal*," I argued.

"If you really want to heal," said Larry, "write this story. Look at your life from where you are now and it will help you put the pieces together." He encouraged us to get our money back and cancel our slots in the seminar. "Don't sabotage yourselves out of fear," he said. "Wake up! Don't allow this to happen. You've wanted to write this book for many years and the time is NOW!"

So, we cancelled our check to Mr. Wonderful and sent Arbor our signed contract and some money to get started on *I, WITNESS.*

Everything Larry said is true. Writing this book was painful, but it was the pain that comes with cleaning out a festering wound so that, at last, it can heal. He was also right about putting the pieces together. Looking at the puzzle of my life from this vantage point, I saw patterns I'd never seen before. Assembling the pieces, putting them in their proper places, I can at last see the whole picture.

Appendices

Appendix A: Glossary of Watchtower Terminology

apostate – An ex-Witness who speaks out publicly against the organization.

Armageddon – A battle between the forces of God and Satan that the Jehovah's Witnesses believe to be in the near future. During the battle, the wicked on earth will be destroyed and the planet given over to the faithful (the Jehovah's Witnesses) as a paradise in which they will live forever.

auxiliary pioneer – A part time pioneer who puts 60 hours per month into the door-to-door ministry.

Bethelite – A Witness who works at the WTS headquarters in Brooklyn.

disassociation – This occurs when a baptized Witness leaves the congregation on his or her own. Disassociated Witnesses are shunned.

Disfellowshipping – The act of removing a believer from the rolls of the organization for violating certain doctrines of the Watchtower Society. The disfellowshipped member is shunned.

Some things for which a believer could be disfellowshipped have included:

- Associating with the wrong people.
- Going into another faith's sanctuary.
- Celebrating proscribed holidays or birthdays.
- Reporting a rape you couldn't prove or didn't fight strenuously enough.
- Accepting a blood transfusion or organ transplant.
- Marrying a non-believer.
- Associating with an apostate Witness.
- Voting or registering to vote.

Elder – A man who is part of the governing group of a Kingdom Hall. An Elder is recommended for appointment by Elders of his congregation and appointed by the ruling body in Brooklyn, NY. The Elders direct the business of the Hall, give talks, do shepherding calls, and take the lead in field service, coaching the door-to-door teachers and encouraging them. They are considered to have been appointed by God.

faithful and discreet slave – The role the WTS sees for itself in the world. The claim is that Christ returned in the late 1800s and found the Witnesses working and preaching when no one else was. He then is supposed to have said, "Good and faithful servants, because you have been faithful, I shall appoint you over all of my belongings."

field service – The door-to-door ministry.

Holy Spirit – According to the Watchtower Society, this is God's active force in the world. It is the Counselor, or Helper Jesus promised to send in His place after He left the world—the invisible Guide of the Watchtower Society's efforts.

Jehovah's Witness – A sect of Christians who follow the millennial teachings of Charles Taze Russell. Abbreviated as JW. The Witnesses believe that the true name of God and the only name He recognizes is "Jehovah."

ministerial servant – A person who fulfills certain duties within the Kingdom Hall such as working the sound equipment, passing out magazines from the book room, reading at the Watchtower Study, and assisting Elders in shepherding calls.

pioneer – A person dedicated to the field service ministry full time. A full time pioneer puts in 90 hours per month or more.

presiding overseer – A man trained by the WTS to encourage the Elders to do more in the area of field service.

publisher – A person qualified to teach door-to-door. This is a reference to Isaiah 52:7: "How comely upon the mountains are the feet of the one bringing good news, the one *publishing peace…*"

shepherding calls – Calls made by Elders at the homes of members who are not attending meetings regularly or participating in the door-to-door ministry.

The Watchtower **and** *Awake* – Bi-weekly magazines published by the Watchtower Society for the edification of Witnesses and the general public. They are written by the Bethelite staff of the Watchtower Bible and Tract Society.

Watchtower Bible and Tract Society – Originally *Bible Students* which was founded by Charles Taze Russell in 1881. It is the driving force behind the doctrines of the Kingdom Hall of Jehovah's Witnesses and the publisher of The Watchtower and Awake! magazines. Its headquarters are in Brooklyn, NY. Abbreviated as WTS.

Appendix B: Meetings to be Attended by Jehovah's Witnesses

Congregational Meetings

These are open to the public and held three times a week. The meetings are synchronized so that all congregations are studying the same material at the same meeting from the most recent publications. Meetings of Jehovah's Witnesses open and close with prayer, and hymns are sung at Kingdom Hall meetings, as well as at assemblies and conventions. Dress for meetings is local business attire—i.e., in the US, a suit and tie for men, and conservative dresses/skirts for females—pants are considered inappropriate for meetings.

Theocratic Ministry School

Theocratic Ministry School is held on a weekday evening. The School is designed to train publishers to be more effective in their ministry. Publishers are trained in the use of the Bible and the meetings concentrate on the reading of the entire Bible over a period of time. The believers practice giving short public talks, do Bible research, and role-play presenting material to people one might meet in the field service. Enrolment is voluntary and open to all congregation members in good standing.

Service Meeting

The Service Meeting is a training program for preaching work. It gives the believers instructions on how to be more efficient in their door-to-door ministry. *Our Kingdom Ministry* is a monthly publication used during Service Meetings.

Public Talk

At this meeting an Elder or ministerial servant delivers a discourse on a Biblical subject. The speaker may be from the local congregation or from a neighboring Kingdom Hall. This is generally held on Sundays, but may be on another day if that is more convenient. The talk focuses on interested members of the public who are not Jehovah's Witnesses.

Watchtower Study

Following the Public Talk is the Watchtower Study. The Bible is studied using an article in *The Watchtower* magazine as a reference. An experienced Elder leads the discussion from the dais and poses questions from the article to the gathering after the reading of each paragraph, then asks review questions at the end of an article. The Public Talk and Watchtower Study together usually last 2 hours.

Book Study

Congregational Book Study is a separate meeting held during the week for which Witnesses meet in groups of about 10 to 15, usually in private homes. Spiritual topics are covered using a study book or a brochure from the Watchtower Society. This is similar in format to the Watchtower Study, but the meeting format is less formal and more interactive. The Elder who serves as book study facilitator is often responsible for 'shepherding' believers who attend it and for organizing and conducting field service meetings.